Starting English
A beginner's course

Joanna Gray

CASSELL

CASSELL Publishers Ltd.
Villiers House, 41-47 Strand, London, WC2N 5JE

ISBN 0 304 31325 4

First published 1981
This edition first published 1986
Reprinted 1987, 1988, 1989, 1991

Acknowledgements

The authors and Publishers are grateful to the following for permission to use photographs in this book.
Ace Photo Agency p.3; Fotobank pp.6,27 and 56; Barnaby's Picture Library p.9; The British Tourist Authority pp.10, 29, 43, 44, 56 and 114; Sporting Pictures UK Ltd p.15; Camera Press p.33; Kodak p.40; Pentax p.40; National Motor Museum p.42; Colorific pp.51 and 95; P. & P. F. James p.75; Telefocus pp.115 and 116.

Thanks also to *Guardian Newspapers* and *The Mirror Group* for permission to reproduce their front pages on p.39 and to *Littlewoods* for the catalogue pages on p.23.

Illustrations by:
John Plumb, Bob Warburton and Ted Draper

Designer David Noble
DP Press, Sevenoaks, Kent

Typeset by Phoenix Photosetting
Chatham, Kent.

Printing and bound in Hong Kong by Wing King Tong Co., Ltd.

Contents

Introduction

You are starting to learn English. This new *Starting English* will help you to learn in colour. The illustrations will also help you to enjoy learning English.

Of course you need to learn grammar. The grammar in this book will make it easier for you to say what you really mean and to understand what other people say.

We know that you want to talk about yourself, your friends and the things around you and the book helps you to do this. Then it helps you to say 'yes' or 'no' to invitations, to ask someone how to get somewhere and how to tell the time.

Of course this is not enough. You want to talk about yesterday, today and tomorrow, and the book shows you how to do this too.

If you want to use your English, you will have to learn a lot of new words. You will also have to learn to agree and disagree, to use the telephone, to ask for things, to apologise when you make a mistake and to do it all in English.

You will soon be able to read and understand a short piece of written English and by the end of the book you will be able to understand the news on television or radio and write a letter in English. You will never be lost when you are with English-speaking people and you will have plenty of practice in listening to, reading and writing English.

This book will help you to do all these things. But you will also have to work at home; reading the book is not enough.

I should like to thank Michael Thorn for his contributions and advice throughout the preparation of this book and Joy McKellen for her very useful editorial help.

Now it's up to you. Enjoy yourself. . . .

London 1985   *Joanna Gray*

Hello, I'm Robert

DIALOGUE

ROBERT	Hello, I'm Robert. What's your name?
SYLVIA	My name's Sylvia.
ROBERT	Are you French?
SYLVIA	No, I'm not, I'm Swiss.

A Practise with another student.

ROBERT	Hello, I'm —. What's your name?
SYLVIA	My name's —.
ROBERT	Are you —?
SYLVIA	No, I'm not, I'm —.

B Look at this conversation.

ROBERT	Are you married?
SYLVIA	No, I'm not.
ROBERT	Are you a student?
SYLVIA	Yes, I am.

Answer the questions with: 'Yes, I am' or 'No, I'm not'.

1 Are you married?   **3** Are you French?
2 Are you a student?   **4** Are you Swiss?

C Here are the letters:

Aa, Bb, Cc, Dd, Ee, Ff, Gg, Hh, Ii, Jj, Kk,
Ll, Mm, Nn, Oo, Pp, Qq, Rr, Ss, Tt, Uu,
Vv, Ww, Xx, Yy, Zz.

Look at this conversation:

TEACHER	What's your name?
SYLVIA	Sylvia Moser.
TEACHER	Can you spell that please?
SYLVIA	S–Y–L–V–I–A M–O–S–E–R

Practise the conversation. Use your name.

D Learn the numbers.

1 = one	5 = five	9 = nine	13 = thirteen	17 = seventeen
2 = two	6 = six	10 = ten	14 = fourteen	18 = eighteen
3 = three	7 = seven	11 = eleven	15 = fifteen	19 = nineteen
4 = four	8 = eight	12 = twelve	16 = sixteen	20 = twenty

Now do the following sums:

Example: 3 + 2 make . . . three plus two make five

1　3 + 2 make . . .　　　　**5**　11 + 9 make . . .　　　　**9**　18 + 1 make . . .
2　8 + 5 make . . .　　　　**6**　14 + 2 make . . .　　　　**10**　14 + 3 make . . .
3　6 + 4 make . . .　　　　**7**　17 + 3 make . . .
4　7 + 8 make . . .　　　　**8**　19 + 1 make . . .

LISTENING ACTIVITIES

E　Look at the boxes.

Listen to the numbers.
Put the numbers you hear in the boxes. Then add the numbers.

Example:　　**A**　　　　　　　　**B**　　　　　　　　**C**

1　[　　] + [　　] + [　　]　make _____

2　[　　] + [　　] + [　　]　make _____

Now listen again and check with your neighbours. Are your answers right?

Practice:　　**A**　　　　　　　　**B**　　　　　　　　**C**

1　[　　] + [　　] + [　　]　make _____

2　[　　] + [　　] + [　　]　make _____

3　[　　] + [　　] + [　　]　make _____

Now listen again and check your answers.

READING COMPREHENSION

Gudrun is German. She's nineteen years old.
She's slim and fair and not very tall. She's a secretary.
She's not married.

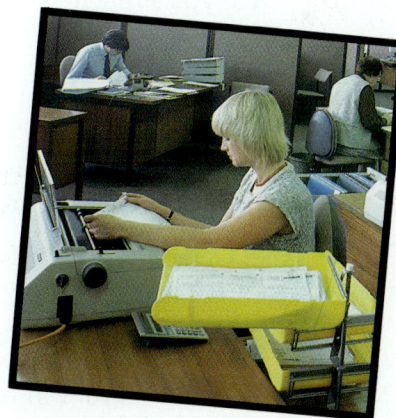

F　Look at these conversations:

'Is Gudrun French?'　　　　'Is she German?'
'No, she's not.'　　　　　　'Yes, she is.'

Answer the following questions about Gudrun:

1　Is she French?　　　　　　6　Is she dark?
2　Is she German?　　　　　　7　Is she fair?
3　Is she eighteen years old?　8　Is she tall?
4　Is she nineteen years old?　9　Is she married?
5　Is she slim?　　　　　　　10　Is she a secretary?

3

GRAMMAR SUMMARY

G Note the *simple present* form of the verb *to be:*

I am (I'm) You are (you're) He/she/it is (he's, she's, it's)	Scottish.
We are (we're) You are (you're) They are (they're)	small.

This is how we form negatives:

I am (I'm) You are (You're) He/she/it is (he's, she's, it's)	not	French.
We are (we're) You are (you're) They are (they're)		tall.

And this is how we ask questions:

Am I Are you Is he (is she, is it)	Scottish?
Are we Are you Are they	small?

We answer questions like this:

Yes, I am. No, I'm not. Yes, he is. No, he's not.

Example: 'Are you French?'   'Is he Swiss?'
          'Yes, I am,'   'Yes, he is,'
          or 'No I'm not.'   or 'No, he's not.'

H   Look at these conversations:

Is she fair?   Are you Swiss?
Yes, she is.   No, I'm not.

Now you make questions with **to be.**

1 — French   4 — tall?   7 — a student?
  Yes, I am.   Yes, he is.   Yes, she is.
2 — Swiss?   5 — a student?   8 — French?
  No, she's not.   No, I'm not.   Yes, they are.
3 — married?   6 — tall?
  Yes, they are.   No, she's not.

I   Look at these conversations:

Is he German?   Are they French?
No, he's not.   No, they're not.

*Answer these questions. Begin your answers with **No, . . .***

1 Is she German?   5 Are they German?
2 Is he tall?   6 Is she Swiss?
3 Are they Swiss?   7 Are you married?
4 Are you French?   8 Is Sylvia French?

HOMEWORK EXERCISES

A   Answer the following questions:

1 Are you Swiss?   4 Are you married?
2 Are you fair?   5 Are you tall?
3 Are you a student?

B   Write these numbers:

Example: 9: nine   11: eleven

| **1** 8 | **3** 14 | **5** 19 | **7** 3 | **9** 15 |
| **2** 12 | **4** 17 | **6** 2 | **8** 5 | **10** 18 |

C   Daniel says:

My name is Daniel. I'm twenty-nine years old and I'm French. I'm tall and fair. I'm married. I'm a teacher.
Now write about yourself.

D   Dictation

My name is Robert. I am eighteen years old and I am French. I am not married. Sylvia is small and fair. She is seventeen and she is a student.

STUDY THE WORDS

Remember these words (look at the Dialogue):

Nationalities:
French: He is French.
          He is from France.

Swiss: He is Swiss.
          He is from Switzerland.

German: He is German.
          He is from Germany.

Scottish: He is Scottish.
          He is from Scotland.

Occupations:
student   teacher
secretary

Remember these words (look at the Reading comprehension):

People:
slim   dark   small
fair   tall   married

Other words and phrases in this unit (can you find them?):

What's your name? My name's Robert.

Where do you come from?

DIALOGUE

RONNIE   Where do you come from?
SUSIE   From Switzerland.
RONNIE   What do you do?
SUSIE   I work in a travel agency.
RONNIE   Do you? I work in a bank.

A   Practise the conversation.

B   Look at this part of the conversation:

RONNIE   What do you do?
SUSIE   I work in a travel agency.
RONNIE   Do you? I work in a bank.

Here are some more places that people work in:

A supermarket, a hotel, a department store, a shoe shop, an office, a chemist's.

Now have more conversations:

1   RONNIE   What do you do?
    SUSIE   — supermarket.
    RONNIE   — hotel.
2   RONNIE   What do you do?
    SUSIE   — department store.
    RONNIE   — office.
3   RONNIE   What do you do?
    SUSIE   — shoe shop.
    RONNIE   — department store.
4   RONNIE   What do you do?
    SUSIE   — hotel.
    RONNIE   — travel agency.
5   RONNIE   What do you do?
    SUSIE   — office.
    RONNIE   — shoe shop.
6   RONNIE   What do you do?
    SUSIE   — bank.
    RONNIE   — hotel.

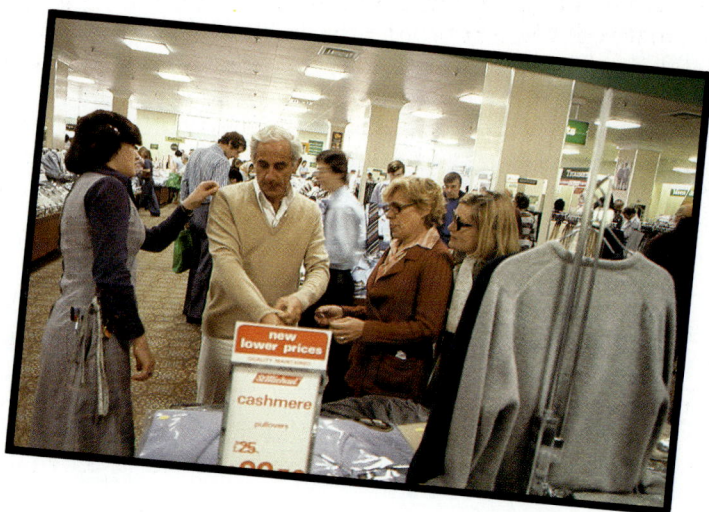

C   Susie says:

I come from Switzerland. I'm Swiss.

Here are some more countries. What does a person from each of these countries say?

1 Germany: German
2 France: French
3 Italy: Italian
4 Spain: Spanish
5 Holland: Dutch
6 Brazil: Brazilian

7 Sweden: Swedish
8 Venezuela: Venezuelan
9 Greece: Greek
10 Where do you come from?
   What do you say?

D   Two businessmen are talking:

A Where do you come from?
B From Rome.

A Who do you work for?
B For Fiat.

Fiat is a big firm. Here are some more big firms.
Rome is a big city. Think of some more big cities.

Rome	Fiat
_____	Nestlé
_____	Ford
_____	IBM
_____	Shell
_____	Cadbury/Schweppes

Practise the conversation.

READING COMPREHENSION

My name is Regine. I'm German. I live in a small town. I'm not married. I live at home with my mother and father, my sister Heidi and my brother Rolf. I work in a department store. I sell writing paper, envelopes, ballpens, pencils and coloured postcards.

I walk to work every morning. I don't work on Saturday afternoon or Sunday and I have a three week holiday in the summer.

E   You are Regine. Answer the questions.

1 What is your name?
2 Where do you come from?
3 Where do you work?
4 Do you sell envelopes?
5 Do you walk to work?
6 Do you work on Saturday afternoon?
7 Do you have a holiday in the summer?
8 What is your sister's name?

F   Regine says:

I have a *mother* and a *father* and one *sister* and one *brother*.

Talk about your family.

LISTENING ACTIVITIES

G   Look at picture A.
Listen to the question and tick the Yes box or the No box. ✓

Does she work in a travel agency?

	Yes	No
A		

Now look at picture B. Listen and tick Yes or No.

Does he work in a shoe shop?

	Yes	No
B		

Check your answers and look at more pictures. Tick the correct box. Listen:

	Yes	No
C		

	Yes	No
E		

	Yes	No
G		

	Yes	No
I		

	Yes	No
D		

	Yes	No
F		

	Yes	No
H		

	Yes	No
J		

Now listen again, look at the pictures, and check your answers.

GRAMMAR SUMMARY

H **Note the *simple present* form:**

to work   I *work* in a department store.
            I *don't work* in a hotel.
            Do you work in an office?

to walk   I *walk* to work every morning.
            I *don't walk* to the bank every day.
            Do you walk to work?

to live   I *live* in a small town.
            I *don't live* in a big town.
            Do you live in a big town?

to have   I *have* a holiday in the summer.
            I *don't have* a holiday in the winter.
            Do you have a holiday in the winter?

to sell   I *sell* envelopes.
            I *don't sell* shoes.
            Do you sell postcards?

Note also the question words *where*, *what* and *who*.

Where do you come from?   What do you sell?
Where do you live?   Who do you work for?
What do you do?

We answer questions like this:

'Yes, I do.' 'No, I don't.'

Examples

'Do you walk to work?'   'Do you live in the city?'
'Yes, I do.'   'No, I don't.'

Prepositions
Note: I live *at home*.
       I work *in* a department store.
       I walk *to* work.
       I don't work *on* Saturday.
       I come *from* Germany.
       I work *for* Fiat.

I **Look at this pattern:**

work/in a hotel
Do you work in a hotel?

Ask more questions.

1 live /in a hotel
2 walk /to work
3 have /a holiday in the winter
4 sell /writing paper
5 work /on Saturday afternoon
6 live /in a small town
7 sell /ballpens
8 work /in an office
9 walk /to school
10 sell /envelopes

J Look at this pattern:

walk /to work
I don't walk to work

Make more negatives.

1 have /a holiday in the winter
2 work /in a travel agency
3 live /in Holland
4 sell /postcards
5 live /at home with my parents
6 work /in an office
7 come from /Greece
8 sell /ballpens
9 work /in a bank
10 have /a six week holiday in the summer

K Put *at, in, to, on, for* or *from* in the spaces.

1 I live — a big town.
2 I walk — the shop every morning.
3 Regine is — home today.
4 I don't work — Saturday afternoon.
5 I work — Nestlé.
6 Do you come — Switzerland?

HOMEWORK EXERCISES

A Regine says:

'I don't work on Saturday afternoon . . .'

Make sentences like this:

Example: live in New York/London
        I don't live in New York. I live in London.

1 work in a bank/department store
2 come from England/ . . .
3 live in a big town/small town
4 have a holiday in the winter/summer
5 sell postcards/shoes

B Now ask questions. You are talking to Miss Fox. She works in a big shop.

Example: You want to know if she walks home from work.

    Do you walk home from work?

1 You want to know if she lives in the town.
2 You want to know if she goes to work by car.
3 You want to know if she sells books.
4 You want to know if she sells coloured pencils.
5 You want to know if she has a holiday in the winter.
6 You want to know if she works on Saturday afternoon.

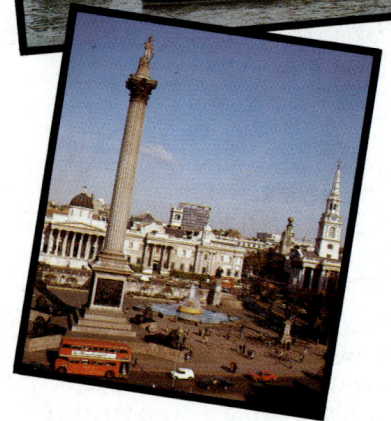

C   Hans comes from Germany. He says:

'I'm German.'

What do these people say?

1 Pierre. He comes from France.
2 Els. She comes from Holland.
3 Carmen. She comes from Spain.
4 Lisa. She comes from Sweden.
5 Maria. She comes from Italy.

D   Dictation

My name is Daniel. I am French. I live in a small town.
   I work in a hotel, but I do not live in the hotel. I live with
my parents. My home is near the hotel, so I walk to work
every day.

STUDY THE WORDS

Remember these words (look at the Dialogue):

Nationalities:

Brazilian:	He is Brazilian: he comes from Brazil.
Dutch:	He is Dutch: he comes from Holland.
Egyptian:	He is Egyptian: he comes from Egypt.
Italian:	He is Italian: he comes from Italy.
Spanish:	He is Spanish: he comes from Spain.
Swedish:	He is Swedish: he comes from Sweden.

The family:

My parents
My brother
My sister

Places people work:

travel agency	department store
bank	shoe shop
supermarket	office
hotel	chemist

**Remember these words
(look at the Reading comprehension):**

writing paper
envelope
ballpen
pencil
postcard

Other words in this unit (can you find them?):

where	winter
home	a holiday
big	a week
near	the morning
far	the afternoon
summer	every day

Days of the week:

Monday	Friday
Tuesday	Saturday
Wednesday	Sunday
Thursday	

Who's that girl over there?

TONY   Who's that girl over there?
GEORGE   Which one?
TONY   The tall one with fair hair.
GEORGE   That's Lisa.
TONY   She's nice, isn't she?

A   Tony wants to know about Lisa.

He says: 'The tall one with fair hair.'

A girl can be: *small, dark, slim* or *big* and some girls have *brown hair*, others have *black hair*.

*Practise George and Tony's conversation. Use other words instead of **tall** and **fair**.*

1   TONY   Who's that girl over there?
    GEORGE   Which one?
    TONY   The — one with — hair.
    GEORGE   That's Brenda.
2   Talk about Mary.
3   Talk about Kathy.

We can talk about boys too.

4   Talk about Don.
5   Talk about Peter.
6   Talk about David.

B   Look at these conversations:

TONY   Who's that girl over there?
GEORGE   That's Lisa.
TONY   She's nice, isn't she?
    Where does she work?
GEORGE   In a travel agency.
KATHY   Who's that boy over there?
BRENDA   That's Tony.
KATHY   He's nice, isn't he?
    Where does he work?
BRENDA   In a bookshop.

Now talk about these people:

1 Brenda. She works in a bank.
2 Kathy. She works in a supermarket.
3 Tom. He works in a bookshop.
4 Roger. He works in an office.
5 Sylvia. She works in a bank.
6 Peter. He works in a record shop.
7 David. He works in a hotel.
8 Emily. She works in a shoe shop.

C Look carefully at these ideas:

'She's nice, isn't she?'
'He's nice, isn't he?'

Complete these sentences with **'isn't she?'** *or* **'isn't he?'**

1 She's nice, — ?
2 Tony's big, — ?
3 Lisa's Swedish, — ?
4 Peter's tall, — ?

5 Brenda's slim, — ?
6 Mary's tall, — ?
7 Kathy's nice, — ?
8 George is small, — ?

D Look at this conversation:

'Where does Lisa come from?'
'From Sweden.'

Ask more questions like this:

1 Where — Carmen — — ?
  From Spain.
2 Where — Maria live?
  In Italy.
3 Where — Peter — ?
  In a record shop.
4 What — Regine — ?
  Writing paper, envelopes and postcards.
5 Where — Sylvia — ?
  In a bank.

E Now look at this conversation:

'Who is that girl?'
'Lisa.'

Ask more questions with **is.**

1 Who — that boy?
  Roger.
2 Where — the car?
  In the car park.
3 Where — Peter now?
  In France.

4 What — that place?
  A hotel.
5 Where — Carmen?
  In the record shop.

F   Look at this conversation:

PETER   Do you sell much writing paper?
REGINE   Yes, I sell a lot.
PETER   Do you sell many envelopes?
REGINE   Yes, I sell a lot.

Take the parts of Peter and Regine and practise the conversation.

1 writing paper
2 envelopes
3 coloured postcards

4 typing paper
5 ballpens
6 pencils

LISTENING ACTIVITIES

G 1   Look at the map and say:

Germany .. Italy . . France.
What number is Italy?

What number is France?
What number is Germany?

Look at the map and find number 4.
Then say the name of the country.
Now do the same with number 5, number 6, number 7,
number 8, number 9 and number 10.

Now listen to some people at an international conference.
Listen again.

Lisa says, 'I come from Germany. I'm German.'
Tony says, 'I come from Italy. I'm Italian.'
Francoise says, 'I come from France. I'm French.'

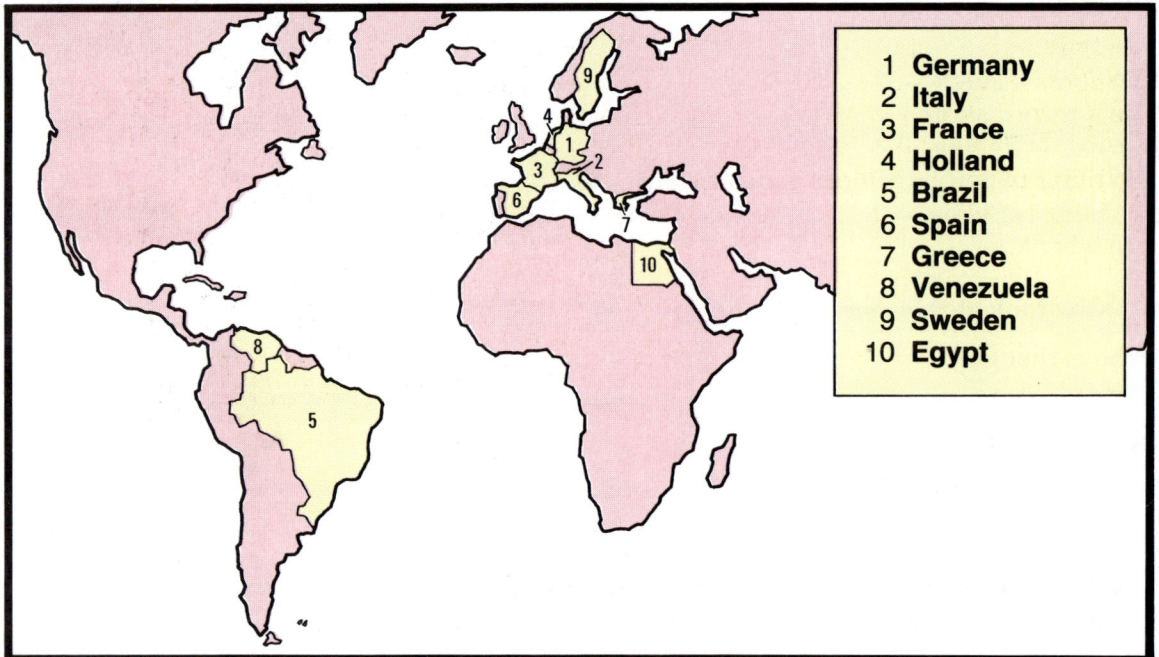

1 **Germany**
2 **Italy**
3 **France**
4 **Holland**
5 **Brazil**
6 **Spain**
7 **Greece**
8 **Venezuela**
9 **Sweden**
10 **Egypt**

2   Write the countries and the nationalities of Carmen, Hans, George, Ingrid, Maria, Skouros and Ahmad.

Name	Country	Nationality
1 Lisa	Germany	German
2 Tony	Italy	Italian
3 Francoise	France	French
4 Carmen		
5 Hans		
6 George		
7 Ingrid		
8 Maria		
9 Skouros		
10 Ahmad		

READING COMPREHENSION

My name is David Thomas. I'm twenty-four and I come from Wales, but now I live in Greenwich. I travel to London by train every day. I work in a big shop. I buy and sell antique furniture. I also write for a magazine called *Antiques Monthly*. I like my job very much. I don't work on Saturday or Sunday. Every Saturday I play rugby.

H   Questions

 1 How old is David?
 2 Where does he come from?
 3 Where does he live now?
 4 How does he travel to London?
 5 Where does he work?
 6 What does he do?
 7 Does he like his job?
 8 What magazine does he write for?
 9 Does he work on Saturday?
10 What does he do on Saturday?

I   Now ask David some questions.

Example: Ask how old he is.
          How old are you?

1 Ask how old he is.
2 Ask where he comes from.
3 Ask where he lives now.
4 Ask how he travels to work.
5 Ask where he works.
6 Ask if he likes his job.
7 Ask what magazine he writes for.
8 Ask what he does on a Saturday.

GRAMMAR SUMMARY

J Note the _s_ on the he/she/it form of the _simple present_:

Where _does_ he/she _work_?
He/she _works_ in a bank.
He/she _doesn't work_ in a hotel.

To make statements

I You	work	
He/she	works	in a bank.
We You They	work	

To make questions

Do	I you		
Does	he/she	work	in a bank?
Do	we you they		

To make negatives

I You	don't (do not)		
He/she	doesn't (does not)	work	in a hotel.
We You They	don't (do not)		

Notice how we ask questions using **to be.**

Who's (who is) that girl?
Where's (where is) that girl?
What's (what is) that record?
How old is she?
What colour is her hair?

Note: _much, many, a lot of._

Do you buy	_much_ _many_	writing paper? envelopes?
Yes, I buy	_a lot of_	writing paper. envelopes.
There isn't There aren't	_much_ _many_	writing paper. envelopes.

K Fill in the questionnaire.

Put a tick in the Yes box or the No box	Yes	No
1 Do you come from London?		
2 Do you live in a big town?		
3 Do you work on Saturday?		
4 Do you read many books?		
5 Do you read a newspaper every day?		
6 Do you walk a lot?		
7 Do you have a holiday in the summer?		
8 Do you have a holiday in the winter?		
9 Do you have any brothers or sisters?		
10 (a) Do you play tennis?		
(b) Do you play football?		
(c) Do you swim?		

Change questionnaires and tell the class about each other:

Example: Peter doesn't come from London. He lives in a big town. He doesn't work on Saturday, but he reads a lot of books, etc.

HOMEWORK EXERCISES

A Complete the conversation, putting one word in place of each blank.

TONY   Who — that girl?
GEORGE   — one?
TONY   The — one with — hair.
GEORGE   That's Meg.
TONY   — — she — from?
GEORGE   Liverpool.
TONY   She's very nice, — n't she? Where — — work?
GEORGE   She — in the bookshop near the bank.

B Look at this pattern:

Pierre is French.
He comes from France.

Where do these people come from?

1 Sylvia is Swiss. She . . .
2 Maria is Brazilian. She . . .
3 Ele is Dutch. She . . .
4 Orestes is Greek. He . . .
5 Carlo is Italian. He . . .

C   George comes from Wales. He is twenty-four years old. Now he lives near Oxford. He works at a bookshop in the centre of Oxford. He sells old books and he knows a lot about them. He is tall and slim and he has dark hair and brown eyes. He writes about old books for a magazine called *Rare Books*.

Now ask questions about George.

1 Ask where George comes from.
2 Ask how old he is.
3 Ask where he lives.
4 Ask where he works.
5 Ask what he sells.
6 Ask what colour his eyes are.
7 Ask what he writes about.
8 Ask what magazine he writes for.

D   **Write answers to your questions about George.**

E   **Dictation**

The tall boy with fair hair is eighteen years old and he comes from Sweden. He works in a record shop.

The small boy with dark hair is seventeen. He is Spanish, but he does not live in Spain. He lives in France. He works in a hotel.

STUDY THE WORDS

Remember these words (look at the Dialogue):

People:
who
which
hair
brown
black
nice

Places:
bookshop
record shop
car park

Remember these words (look at the Reading comprehension):

Games:
football
rugby
tennis

Other words in this unit (can you find them?):

furniture
antique
magazine
newspaper
typing paper
job
colour

Is there any sugar?

DIALOGUE

SOPHIE   Here's some coffee.
GEORGE   Oh, fantastic . . . er . . . is there any sugar?
SOPHIE   Sugar . . . yes, of course . . . here you are.
GEORGE   Thanks . . . er . . .
SOPHIE   What's the matter now?
GEORGE   Er . . . are there any chocolate biscuits?
SOPHIE   No, there aren't.
GEORGE   Oh . . .

A   Questions

1 Does Sophie bring George any tea?
2 Does she bring him any coffee?
3 Does she bring him any sugar?
4 Does she bring him any chocolate biscuits?
5 Why is George pleased? Because Sophie brings him
   some —.
6 Why isn't he pleased? Because there aren't any — —.

B   Sophie has these things in her kitchen:

coffee, tea, sugar, jam, butter, milk and salt.

Learn them and have conversations like this:

GEORGE   Is there any sugar?
SOPHIE   Yes, (of course) there is.
GEORGE   Is there any (more) coffee?
SOPHIE   No, (I'm afraid) there isn't.

C   Sophie could say:

'There's some sugar in the kitchen.'

Make more sentences like this.

1 tea   4 milk
2 jam   5 salt
3 butter   6 coffee

19

D   Sophie also has these things in her kitchen:

biscuits, apples, oranges, eggs, sausages and tomatoes.

Learn them and have conversations like this:

GEORGE   Are there any oranges?
SOPHIE   Yes, (of course) there are.
GEORGE   Are there any biscuits?
SOPHIE   No, (I'm afraid) there aren't.

E   Sophie could say:

'There are some biscuits in the kitchen.'

Make more sentences like this.

1 biscuits   4 tomatoes
2 eggs   5 apples
3 oranges   6 sausages

F   Learn these numbers:

21 twenty-one	26 twenty-six	31 thirty-one	60 sixty
22 twenty-two	27 twenty-seven	32 thirty-two	70 seventy
23 twenty-three	28 twenty-eight	40 forty	80 eighty
24 twenty-four	29 twenty-nine	41 forty-one	90 ninety
25 twenty-five	30 thirty	50 fifty	100 a hundred

Look at the price list.

Sophie is in the shop.

SOPHIE   I'd like some apples and some biscuits, please.
ASSISTANT   Thank you. That's 28p and 26p . . . 54p, please.

Practise the conversation. (You only have a pound!)

G   Now practise using *much, many* and *a lot of*. You are going shopping, so you look in your kitchen. You have:

milk	4 bottles	biscuits	a kilo
butter	a small piece	apples	2
coffee	very little	tomatoes	16
tea	half a packet	eggs	3

Have conversations:

Example: A   Is there much butter?
         B   No, not much.
         A   Is there much milk?
         B   Yes, there's a lot.
         A   Are there many biscuits?
         B   Yes, there are a lot.
         A   Are there many eggs?
         B   No, not many.

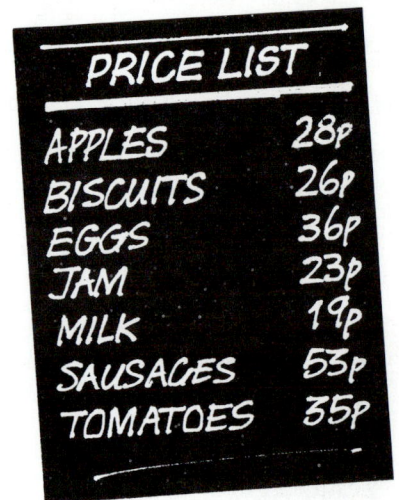

PRICE LIST	
APPLES	28p
BISCUITS	26p
EGGS	36p
JAM	23p
MILK	19p
SAUSAGES	53p
TOMATOES	35p

READING COMPREHENSION

When my brother wants to buy a new suit he goes to the bank and he gets some money. Then he walks from shop to shop looking in the windows. When he sees a suit he likes, he goes in and buys it.

   I don't buy my suits this way. I look at the pictures in my mail order catalogue and send my order by post. A few days later the postman brings me a parcel. I don't pay at once. I send a little money every week.

H   Questions

 1 Where does my brother go to get some money?
 2 What does he do when he has the money?
 3 What does he do when he sees a suit that he likes?
 4 Does the writer walk from shop to shop?
 5 What does he look at?
 6 How does he order his new clothes?
 7 What does the postman bring?
 8 What do you think is in the parcel?
 9 Does the writer pay at once?
10 How does he pay?

GRAMMAR SUMMARY

I Note:

Is there Are there	*any*	tea, sugar, jam, biscuits, apples	in the kitchen?
There is There are	*some*	sugar biscuits	in the kitchen.
There isn't There aren't	*any*	sugar biscuits	in the kitchen.

Note the prepositions:

They buy their clothes *in* shops.
They go *to* the bank.
They go *into* the shop.
I look *at* the pictures.
I order my new clothes *by* post.
I send money every week *for* twenty weeks.

Note: A *few* days later the postman brings a parcel.
       I send *a little* money every week.

We say: A *few* biscuits   *A little* tea
          A *few* apples   *A little* jam

J Talk about the things in the Easyway mail order catalogue.

Here is the Index to the Easyway mail order catalogue:

Examples:

There are some (lovely) sweaters for men in the catalogue.

(Oh, dear) There aren't any books in the catalogue.

Are there any shoes in the catalogue?
Yes there are.

Are there any cameras in the catalogue?
No, there aren't.

Not in the catalogue:

books
records
cameras
radios

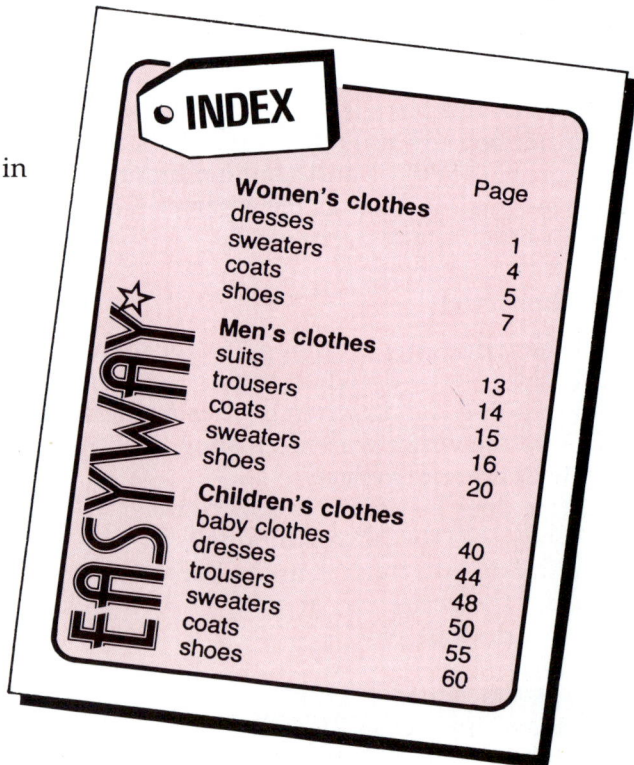

INDEX	
Women's clothes	**Page**
dresses	1
sweaters	4
coats	5
shoes	7
Men's clothes	
suits	13
trousers	14
coats	15
sweaters	16
shoes	20
Children's clothes	
baby clothes	40
dresses	44
trousers	48
sweaters	50
coats	55
shoes	60

EASYWAY

LISTENING ACTIVITIES

K Now listen to this advertisement.

*Look at your Easyway mail order catalogue.
Listen again. Fill in the list.*

Index	Page
Women's sweaters	4
Women's shoes	7
Men's suits	13
Women's coats	
Men's coats	
Children's coats	
Men's trousers	
Baby clothes	
Children's dresses	
Men's sweaters	
Children's shoes	

HOMEWORK EXERCISES

A   Put *some* or *any* in the spaces.

1 There's — tea in the kitchen.
2 There isn't — sugar.
3 Is there — coffee?

4 There's — butter in the kitchen.
5 Is there — jam?
6 Are there — biscuits?

B   Put *much, many* or *a lot of* in the spaces.

1 There aren't — sweaters in the catalogue.
2 Are there — coats in the catalogue?
3 There are — lovely shoes in the catalogue.
4 There aren't — cameras in the catalogue.
5 There are — nice suits in the catalogue.
6 How — do you pay every week?

C   Put in the prepositions.

1 Brenda lives — that house.
2 I don't pay for my clothes — once.
3 Come — the kitchen.
4 The parcels come — post.

D   Dictation

There is some sugar, there is some coffee and there is a lot of tea, but there is not much jam. There are some tomatoes, but there are not any eggs or biscuits and there is not much milk.

So we want jam, eggs, biscuits and milk.

STUDY THE WORDS

Remember these words (look at the Dialogue):

Food and drink:

coffee	jam
tea	salt
biscuits	eggs
chocolate	sausages
sugar	tomatoes
milk	oranges
butter	apples

Remember these words (look at the Reading comprehension):

Clothes:

dress	shoes
coat	trousers
sweater	suit

Other words and phrases in this unit (can you find them?):

I'm afraid	radio
what's the matter?	camera
kitchen	few
bottle	lovely
money	fantastic
catalogue	kilo
pictures	pound
postman	order
parcel	

Have you got any envelopes, please?

ASSISTANT	Good afternoon. Can I help you?
GEORGE	Have you got any envelopes, please?
ASSISTANT	Yes, here you are.
GEORGE	Thank you. How much is that?
ASSISTANT	50p please.
GEORGE	Thank you.

A Practise the conversation. You want:

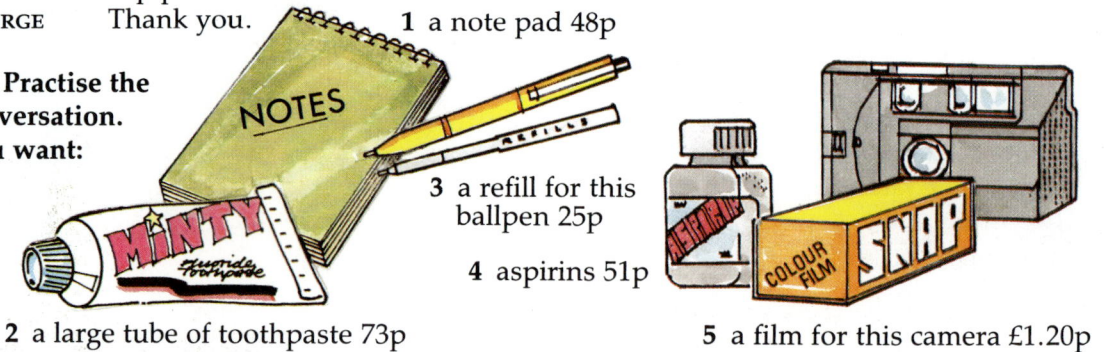

1 a note pad 48p

3 a refill for this ballpen 25p

4 aspirins 51p

2 a large tube of toothpaste 73p

5 a film for this camera £1.20p

B Listen again to George and the assistant.

How much change does George get?
Write the amount in this box.

Now check your answer.

£	p

Listen to George and the assistant at the chemist's.
Write the amounts George spends in these boxes.

£	p

1 A large bottle of aspirins

2 A large tube of toothpaste

3 A film – 20 exposures

4 The shop assistant says:
'Don't forget your change, sir.'
How much change does George get?

C   Look at this conversation:

'Have you got any envelopes, please?'
'I'm afraid we don't sell envelopes.'

Practise the conversation:

1 aspirins
2 a ballpen
3 an English dictionary

4 a French newspaper
5 a 10p stamp
6 a film for this camera

D   George and Brenda are shopping.

GEORGE   Have you got everything now?
BRENDA   I've got the apples but I haven't got the oranges.

Brenda has got: the sugar
the coffee
the tea
the apples
the jam

Brenda hasn't got: the biscuits
the oranges
the eggs
the tomatoes
the butter

Practise the conversation.

READING COMPREHENSION

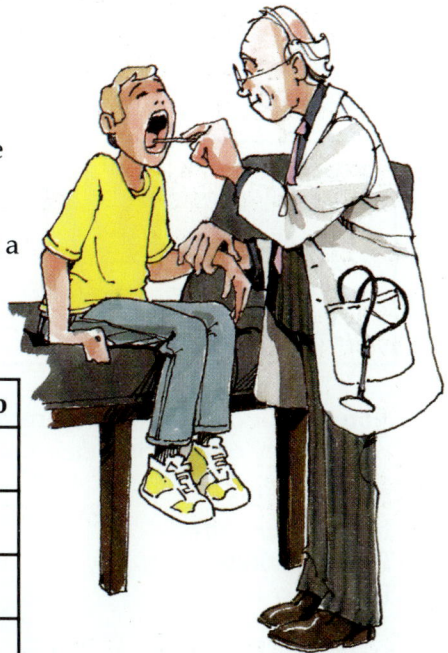

I am a family doctor and I've got about two thousand
patients. A lot of my patients are never ill, so I never see
them. But I've got a lot of old patients, and they often have
problems. They sometimes come to see me two or three
times a week. Then there are the mothers with young
children. They often bring their children to see me. I've got a
very good secretary, but I'm always very busy.

E   Read about the doctor and put a √

Examples:

	Yes	No
The doctor has got fifty patients.		√
The doctor has got about two thousand patients.	√	
1 The doctor is a busy man.		
2 Many of the patients are never ill.		
3 Some of the old people have a lot of problems.		
4 Mothers never bring their children to see the doctor.		
5 The doctor hasn't got a secretary.		

GRAMMAR SUMMARY

F Note: A Have you got a key?
B No, I'm afraid I haven't.
C Don't worry, I've got one.

Questions

Have I Have you Has he, has she Have we Have you Have they	got a key?

Negatives

I haven't You haven't He hasn't, she hasn't We haven't You haven't They haven't	got a key.

Statements

I've You've He's, she's We've You've They've	got a key.

Note: A lot of *my* patients are never ill.
They often bring *their* children to see me.

This is *my* tea.　　　　This is *our* catalogue.
This is *your* coffee.　　This is *your* newspaper.
This is *his* key.　　　　This is *their* car.
This is *her* house.

Note: *never, sometimes, often, usually* **and** *always.*

A lot of my patients are *never* ill.
They *sometimes* come to see me.
They *often* have problems.
The doctor doesn't *usually* see patients on a Sunday.
The doctor is *always* very busy.

Look:

never	0%
sometimes	30%
often	60%
usually	80%
always	100%

G Have a conversation with the doctor.

1 YOU Ask the doctor if he's a very busy man.
   DOCTOR _____

2 YOU Ask how many patients he's got.
   DOCTOR _____

3 YOU Ask if he's got a lot of old patients.
   DOCTOR _____

4 YOU Ask if they often come to see him.
   DOCTOR _____

5 YOU Ask if he's got a secretary.
   DOCTOR _____

6 YOU Ask if she's a good secretary.
   DOCTOR _____

7 YOU Ask if the doctor sees a lot of mothers with young
       children.
   DOCTOR _____

8 YOU Ask if he often visits patients at their homes.
   DOCTOR _____

9 YOU Thank the doctor for speaking to you.

H Put: *my, your, his, her, our, your* or *their* in the spaces.

1 These shoes belong to me. They are — shoes.
2 This coat belongs to Lisa. It's — coat.
3 This car belongs to Frank and Sally. It's — car.
4 We have the tickets for these seats. They are — seats.
5 These records belong to me and my brother. They are —
   records.
6 This is Sally's book. It's — book.
7 The things that belong to you are in the sitting-room. —
   things are in the sitting-room.
8 The car I drive is blue. — car is blue.
9 The car John drives is French. — car is French.
10 George and Vivian have a son of ten. — son is ten years
   old.

I Do you do these things?

never, sometimes, often, usually, always

1 go to the cinema
2 eat at a nice restaurant
3 listen to the radio in the morning
4 go to see your doctor
5 play tennis
6 watch television

A   You are in a shop. You want to buy some postcards. What do you say?

YOU   Have you got any postcards, please?

Continue:

1 You are in a shop. You want to buy some toothpaste. What do you say?

2 You are in a shop and you want to buy a new ballpen. You see a pen you like. Ask the price.

3 You work in a shop that sells postcards. A customer asks for stamps. You don't sell stamps. Tell the customer, politely.

4 You want to make a telephone call. You have a 50p piece. Ask your friend for change. (Use *got*.)

5 You have a ballpen, but you want a refill. You go into the shop. What do you ask the assistant?

B   Ask questions with *got*.

Example: you/oranges
            Have you *got* any oranges?

            she/a ballpen
            Has she *got* a ballpen?

1 you/coffee
2 he/a key
3 we/butter
4 they/stamps
5 you/aspirins

C   Practise using *my, your*, etc.

Example: These shoes belong to me.
            They are my shoes.

1 These shoes belong to my sister.
2 This pen belongs to George.
3 This car belongs to them.
4 These envelopes belong to you.
5 This toothpaste belongs to him.

D   Dictation

There is a small shop at the end of our road. I buy my newspaper there every Sunday. This is the only shop that is open on a Sunday, so it is always very busy.

   They sell milk, eggs, biscuits, tea and coffee. You can get aspirins, toothpaste or a writing pad there. It is a nice little shop.

STUDY THE WORDS

Remember these words (look at the Dialogue):

Things you can buy:
writing pad
refill for a ballpen
film
dictionary

Remember these words (look at the Reading comprehension):

The Doctor:
doctor   aspirins
patients   problem
ill

Other words in this unit (can you find them?):

old	the sitting-room
young	seat
good	ticket
blue	key
busy	cinema
times	restaurant
children	

Here is your first progress test. You and your teacher can
see how much English you know.

1 This is a conversation with a new student, Maria. Read
her answers. Then write your name and the questions you
ask Maria.

YOU   Hello, I'm _____. _____ name?

MARIA   My name's Maria.

YOU   _____ from?

MARIA   I come from Brazil.

YOU   _____ married?

MARIA   No, I'm not married, I'm single.

YOU   _____ ?

MARIA   At home, with my parents

YOU   _____ ?

MARIA   I work in a bank.

2 When does Maria go to work? How does Maria travel to work?
Look at this chart:

	Sunday	Monday	Tuesday	Wednes-day	Thursday	Friday	Saturday
Walks	✕	✓	✓	✓	✕	✓	✕
By train	✕	✕	✕	✕	✕	✕	✕
By bus	✕	✕	✕	✕	✓	✕	✕

Look at the example questions and answers.

QUESTION   Does Maria go to work on Saturday?
ANSWER   No, she doesn't.

QUESTION   Does Maria go to work on Monday?
ANSWER   Yes, she does.

QUESTION   How does Maria travel to work on Monday?
ANSWER   She walks.

Now you write the questions and answers.

1 QUESTION _____ on Sunday?

    ANSWER _____ .

2 QUESTION _____ on Tuesday?

    ANSWER _____ .

3 QUESTION How _____ on Tuesday?

    ANSWER _____ .

4 QUESTION How _____ on Thursday?

    ANSWER _____ .

5 QUESTION _____ by train?

    ANSWER No, _____ .

3 It is Saturday now. Maria always goes shopping on Saturday. Look at her shopping list.

Look at these questions and answers.

QUESTION   Is there much milk?
ANSWER   No, not much.

QUESTION   Are there many apples?
ANSWER   No, not many.

QUESTION   Is there much tea?
ANSWER   Yes, there's a lot.

QUESTION   Are there many tomatoes?
ANSWER   Yes, there are a lot.

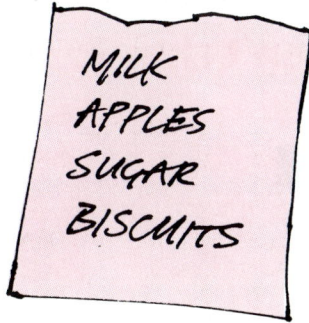

MILK
APPLES
SUGAR
BISCUITS

Now you write questions and answers.

1 QUESTION _____ jam?

  ANSWER Yes, _____ .

2 QUESTION _____ sausages?

  ANSWER No, _____ .

3 QUESTION _____ chocolates?

  ANSWER Yes, _____ .

4 QUESTION _____ tea?

  ANSWER No, _____ .

5 QUESTION _____ eggs?

  ANSWER No, _____ .

4 Answer these questions. Use: *my, his, her, our,* or *their.*

1 QUESTION Does this sweater belong to you?

  ANSWER   Yes, it's _____ sweater.

2 QUESTION Does this shopping list belong to Maria?

  ANSWER   Yes, it's _____ shopping list.

3 QUESTION Does this car belong to George?

  ANSWER   Yes, it's _____ car.

4 QUESTION Do these books belong to us?

  ANSWER   Yes, they are _____ books.

5 QUESTION Do these tickets belong to Frank and Sally?

  ANSWER   Yes, they are _____ tickets.

They're nice, aren't they?

KATHY   Where do you live?
DAVID   Near Victoria station.
KATHY   In a flat or a house?
DAVID   In a flat. Houses are terribly expensive.
KATHY   What's your flat like?
DAVID   It's small and the building is old, but it's
        comfortable. It's very near my office.

A   Questions

1 Where does David live?
2 Does he live in a house?
3 What is the flat like?
4 What is the building like?
5 Do you think he walks to work?

B   Here are some colours:

Red, grey, green, yellow, white, black, brown, blue.

Learn them. Put one colour in each space in the sentences below.

1 Ripe tomatoes are ———.
2 On a sunny day the sky is ———.
3 In summer the leaves on the trees are ———.
4 Ripe bananas are ———.
5 On a rainy day the sky is ———.
6 Tea is ———.
7 Coal is ———.
8 Swans are ———.

C   Learn the adjectives:

young, old, good, bad, etc.

I am *young*, but my grandfather is *old*.
George has a *new* suit. He looks very *nice*.
Nineteen out of twenty is a *good* mark. Three out of twenty
is a *bad* mark.
Elephants are *big*, but baby elephants are *small*.
In Siberia it is very *cold*, but in parts of South America it gets
very *hot*.
Rio is a *long* way from London, but it is only a *short* journey
from London to Paris.
In London the river Thames is *wide*, but some of the streets
in the city are very *narrow*.

D Here is a short list of adjectives:

short, small, narrow, old, hot, long, wide, big.

Put the correct adjective in each space; use each adjective once only.

1 It is very — in India at this time of year.
2 London is a very — city. More than eight million people
   live there.
3 It's a — journey from London to Hong Kong.
4 In Paris the river Seine is — .
5 Roads in the north of Scotland are very — .
6 George can walk to his office. It's only a — journey.
7 My father is — . He doesn't work now.
8 David's flat is very — .

READING COMPREHENSION

I live in a small flat near Victoria station. I have a
sitting-room, a bedroom, a bathroom and a kitchen. The
building is old and dirty, but my flat is clean and the
sitting-room is very comfortable. I have a lot of books and
records and a colour television.
    From my bed I can hear the trains coming into Victoria
station.

E Answer these questions:

1 Where does the writer live?
2 How many rooms has his flat got?
3 What is the building like?
4 Is the flat dirty?
5 What is the sitting-room like?
6 Has the writer got many books?
7 Does the writer like music?
8 Does he watch television?
9 Which room does he sleep in?
10 What can he hear when he is in bed?

F   Note the prepositions:

The television is *near* the window. There are a lot of books *on* the shelves *above* the television, and there's a chair *between* the television and the table. The table is *against* the wall, *under* the window. *Behind* the clock there's a big envelope. So the clock is *in front of* the envelope. I cook my food *in* the kitchen and carry it *from* the kitchen *to* the sitting-room. I eat my dinner *at* the table.

Answer the questions:

1 Where is the television?
2 What are the books on?
3 Where are the shelves?
4 Where is the big envelope?
5 Where is the table?
6 Where does the writer cook his food?
7 Where does he carry it to?
8 Where does he eat it?

GRAMMAR SUMMARY

G   This unit introduces adjectives.

Examples: He's a *big* man.
He has a *small* dog.
He has a *new, yellow* car.

Here is a list of some useful adjectives and their opposites:

big — small	a big dog	tall — short	a tall man
cheap — expensive	a cheap suit	heavy — light	a heavy suitcase
good — bad	a good record	thick — thin	a thick book
hot — cold	a hot day	wide — narrow	a wide road
long — short	a long journey	fast — slow	a fast train
young — old	a young woman	clean — dirty	a clean hotel

Note these useful prepositions:

in, on, at, near, above, under, between, behind, in front of, from, to, by.

I live *in* a small flat.
It's *near* Victoria station.
I park my car *in front of* the house.
The railway is *behind* the house.
The trains run *on* the railway lines.

I go *by* car *from* my flat *to* my office every day.
I work *at* the office till 5.00 pm.
My office is *above* a supermarket.
The supermarket is *between* a shoe shop and a bank.
The supermarket is *under* my office.

LISTENING ACTIVITY

H   Look and listen.

Look at the pictures, first. These people are all English. They
don't live in London but they live near London. The man in
picture 1 is a small man with a big dog, isn't he? Now look at
picture 2. Is the woman in picture 2 small? Is the dog big?
No, of course not. The woman is big and the dog is small.

	Yes	No
1		
3		
5		
7		
9		
2		
4		
6		
8		
10		

I   Revision exercise

1 Think of something that could be *narrow*.
2 What colour are your shoes?
3 Think of something *green*.
4 What colour is the sky in summer?
5 Think of something *big*.
6 Think of something *small*.
7 What could be *short*?
8 What is the opposite of *young*?
9 What could be *heavy*?
10 What is the opposite of *dirty*?
11 Think of a place that gets very *cold* in winter.
12 What's the opposite of *thick*?

HOMEWORK EXERCISES

A   You will need some coloured pens or pencils.

It is summer. A *big* man and a *small* woman are standing in a *green* field, under a *tall* tree. The man is wearing *grey* trousers, a *blue* jacket and *black* shoes. He has *brown* hair. The woman is wearing a *yellow* dress. She has *black* hair. They are looking at a *white* house with a *red* roof.

Draw and colour the picture.

B   Here are some adjectives. Think of something each of them describes.

Example: long – a *long* journey

1 heavy	**5** thick
2 fast	**6** short
3 green	**7** expensive
4 young	**8** dirty

C   Dictation

My grandfather lives with us. He is seventy years old and I like talking to him. Every day I go for a walk with him in the park.
  My grandfather has a dog. The dog's name is Nelson. Nelson is old and he has very short legs and bad eyes. But my grandfather likes him very much.

STUDY THE WORDS

Remember these words (look at the Dialogue and the Reading comprehension):

Buildings	*Nature*
building	tree
house	leaf (leaves)
flat	banana
office	swan
supermarket	dog
window	elephant
shelf	sunny
bedroom	rainy
kitchen	river
bathroom	street
chair	road
table	sky
	coal
	ripe

Other words in this unit (can you find them?):

writer	cold
train	hot
railway	long
lines	short
journey	wide
comfortable	narrow
music	small
television	dirty
new	clean
bad	

They're cheaper in the other shop

Frank wants a new jacket.
He and Sally see some in a shop window.

FRANK   I like that brown one.
SALLY   They're cheaper in the other shop.
FRANK   Yes, these are more expensive, but they're better quality.
SALLY   Let's go in and look at some.

A   Questions

1 Who is with Frank?
2 Where do they see the jacket?
3 What colour is the jacket that Frank likes?
4 What does Sally say about the jackets in the other shop?
5 What does Frank say about the jackets in this shop?

B   Sally says: 'They're cheaper in the other shop.'

Look at the pictures:

Sally says: 'These jackets are cheaper than those.'

Make more comparisons:

1 Frank is tall. Sally is short.
   ____ taller ____ . ____ shorter ____ .
   Frank has long legs. Sally has short legs.
   ____ longer ____ . ____ shorter ____ .

2 Sally is slim, but Brenda is very slim.
   ____ slimmer ____ .

3

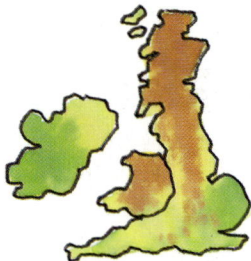

England is big. Wales is small.
____ bigger ____ .
____ smaller ____ .

5

Temperatures today?
India is 30°C. Italy is 22°C.
It's hotter _____ .
It's colder _____ .

7

George's suitcases are light.
Sally's suitcases are heavy.
_____ lighter _____ .
_____ heavier _____ .

4

Jim wears a wide tie.
Henry wears a narrow tie.
____ wider ____ .
____ narrower ____ .

6

Small eggs
26p for six

Big eggs
40p for six

____ more expensive ____
____ cheaper ____

8

Jim's grandfather is 82.
Henry's grandfather is 69.
____ older ____ .
____ younger ____ .

C Look at the pictures

Which suitcase is the cheapest?
Which suitcase is the most expensive?

a small suitcase

a big suitcase

We can say:

The smallest suitcase is the cheapest.
The biggest suitcase is the most expensive.

a very big suitcase

Now look at the pictures of eggs:

small eggs
26p for six

big eggs
40p for six

very big eggs
60p for six

1 Which eggs are the cheapest?
2 Are the big eggs the most expensive?
3 Which eggs are the most expensive?
4 Why are the small eggs the cheapest?
5 Why are the very big eggs the most expensive?

D   Read the conversation.

STUDENT   That's a big newspaper.
TEACHER   Yes, it's *The Guardian*.
STUDENT   Why don't you read *The Mirror*?
TEACHER   I find *The Guardian* more interesting.
STUDENT   Is it more difficult to understand than
          The Mirror?
TEACHER   Yes, it is.
STUDENT   Is it more expensive?
TEACHER   Yes, it's bigger, isn't it?

Compare **The Guardian** and **The Mirror**.

Example: Which is more expensive?
           The Guardian is **more** expensive **than**
           The Mirror.

1 Which is more expensive?
2 Which is more interesting?
3 Which is more difficult to understand?
4 Which is bigger?
5 Why do you think *The Guardian* is more expensive?

LISTENING ACTIVITY

E   Frank and Peter want new bicycles.
Petrol is very expensive so they both want to cycle to work.
They are looking at advertisements.

Listen to their conversation.

Listen again to Frank and Peter. Write the missing words or numbers.

FRANK   What about this Curzon bike? It's very _____ .
        Only _____ .
PETER   Yes, but the Anderson bike is even _____ .
        It's _____ .
FRANK   Hmmm. How _____ is the Anderson one?
PETER   It's a _____ model.
FRANK   The Curzon is a 1979 model. It's _____ .

Frank and Peter are still looking at advertisements. They can't decide which bike to buy.

Now listen to Frank and Peter again. Write the missing words.

PETER   The Anderson bike looks very _____ .
FRANK   Yes, but the Curzon bike looks _____ .
PETER   I don't _____ a big bike. I want a comfortable
        _____ .
FRANK   All right. The Anderson bike is _____ . But the
        Curzon is _____ .

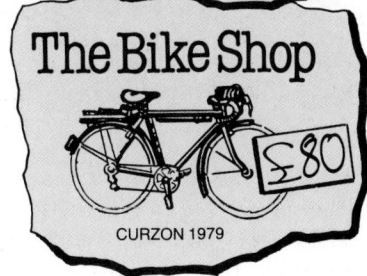

Bike World ★ £65
ANDERSON 1977

The Bike Shop
£80
CURZON 1979

READING COMPREHENSION

I have a cheap plastic camera. On a sunny day I can take good pictures with it. But I can't take good pictures in bad weather and I can't take pictures of moving objects, like a horse or a racing car. The pictures I take indoors with flash aren't very clear.

My brother has a Pentax. His camera is more expensive than mine. It is heavier and it is more complicated. My brother has three lenses for his camera and his photographs are better than mine. He can take good pictures in bad weather, and some of his indoor pictures, taken with flash, are marvellous.

F   Questions

1 Is the writer's camera expensive?
2 Which camera is more expensive?
3 How many lenses do you think the writer's camera has?
4 How many lenses does his brother use?
5 When can the writer take good pictures?
6 Can his brother take photographs in bad weather?
7 Can the writer take pictures indoors with flash?
8 Which camera takes clearer pictures with flash?

G   Compare the Pentax and the plastic camera.

Example: Compare the price.
more expensive

The Pentax is *more expensive than* the plastic camera.

1 Compare the price.   *cheaper*
2 Compare the weight.   *lighter*
3 Compare the weight.   *heavier*
4 Compare the cameras.   *more complicated*
5 Compare the cameras.   *better photographs*

GRAMMAR SUMMARY

H   Comparatives and superlatives

The Victoria Hotel is *big*.
The Victoria hotel is *bigger* than the Park Hotel.
The Victoria hotel is the *biggest* in the town.

Your plan is *complicated*.
Jim's plan is *more complicated*.
Henry's plan is the *most complicated* of the three.

Note:

good — better — best
the *best* shop in the town

bad — worse — worst
the *worst* weather

Note the possessive pronouns:
mine, yours, his, hers, ours, yours, theirs

It's *my* camera.	It's *mine*.
It's *his* camera.	It's *his*.
It's *her* camera.	It's *hers*.
It's *your* camera.	It's *yours*.
It's *our* camera.	It's *ours*.
It's *their* camera.	It's *theirs*.

I **We say:** This is my camera. It's *mine*.
It's Sally's camera. It's *hers*.

Continue:

1 It's Frank's camera. It's _____ .
2 This is Sally's car. It's _____ .
3 This is our house. It's _____ .
4 Those are your shoes. They are _____ .
5 These are my records. They are _____ .
6 This is her watch. It's _____ .
7 This is their car. It's _____ .
8 This is our newspaper. It's _____ .

J **Discussion**

Have you got a camera?
What sort have you got?
What sort of pictures do you like taking?
Do you use different lenses?
Can you explain why we have different lenses and what we
use them for?
Could you bring some of your photographs tomorrow?

HOMEWORK EXERCISES

A **Dictation**

I have a small black and white television and I can get a
good picture. But my brother has got a colour television. It is
bigger, heavier and more complicated than mine. My
brother gets a better picture on his television than I do on
mine. So when there is something very good on TV, I
usually go and see my brother.

B Make comparatives.

1 The USA is (*big*) than Greece.
2 She is (*young*) than her sister.
3 The tomatoes here are (*expensive*) than they are in the supermarket.
4 English is (*easy*) than Japanese.
5 I'm (*tall*) than my brother.
6 This book is (*interesting*) than that one.
7 My cold is (*bad*) than yours.
8 That letter is (*heavy*) than this one.

C Compare these two cars.

1 Compare the price.
2 Which car uses more petrol?
3 Compare the speed they can go.
4 Compare the size.
5 Which car do you like best?
6 Which is the wider car?
7 Compare the length.
8 Which car has the more powerful engine?
9 Which car is easier to park?
10 Which car is noisier?

QUALITY CARS

MORGAN

Maximum speed: 130 m.p.h.
Petrol consumption: 24 m.p.g.
Engine size: 3528 cc
Price: £6,000 approx.

ROLLS-ROYCE SILVER SPIRIT

Maximum speed: 125 m.p.h.
Petrol consumption: 15 m.p.g.
Engine size: 6750 cc
Price: £50,000 approx.

STUDY THE WORDS

Remember these words (look at the Reading comprehension):

The camera:
clear
flash
lens
different
picture
moving object
plastic
marvellous

Other words in this unit (can you find them?):

why   temperature
jacket   quality
tie   petrol
customs   indoors
suitcase   watch
weight   legs
length

Here is a useful list:

small — smaller — smallest
cheap — cheaper — cheapest
hot — hotter — hottest
cold — colder — coldest
long — longer — longest
short — shorter — shortest
young — younger — youngest
old — older — oldest
tall — taller — tallest
clean — cleaner — cleanest
light — lighter — lightest
fast — faster — fastest
slow — slower — slowest
easy — easier — easiest
heavy — heavier — heaviest
dirty — dirtier — dirtiest
expensive — more expensive — most expensive
interesting — more interesting — most interesting
difficult — more difficult — most difficult

Would you like to come to the cinema?

DIALOGUE

KURT	Georgina . . .
GEORGINA	Yes?
KURT	Would you like to come to the cinema this evening?
GEORGINA	Oh, that would be lovely.
KURT	Fine . . . I'll call for you at about six o'clock.

A Questions

1 Ask where Kurt wants to go this evening.
2 Answer the question.
3 Ask who he wants to go with.
4 Answer the question.
5 Does Georgina accept his invitation?
6 What time is Kurt going to call for Georgina?

B Look at this part of the conversation again:

KURT	Would you like to come to the cinema this evening?
GEORGINA	Oh, that would be lovely.

Now practise the conversation, using these words:

1	to the theatre	5	for a drink
2	for a walk in the park	6	to a concert
3	to a football match	7	for a drive
4	to the ballet	8	to a party

C Look at this conversation. Franz also invites Georgina to go out with him.

FRANZ	Would you like to come to the theatre this evening?
GEORGINA	I'm afraid I can't. I'm going to the cinema.

Use the prompts below to make similar sentences:

1	FRANZ	for a walk this afternoon
	GEORGINA	to the cinema
2	FRANZ	to the cinema tomorrow evening
	GEORGINA	to the theatre

3 FRANZ   to the football match this evening
  GEORGINA to a dance
4 FRANZ   to the ballet on Saturday evening
  GEORGINA to a party
5 FRANZ   for a walk in the park tomorrow morning
  GEORGINA for a drive with Kurt
6 FRANZ   to a party on Wednesday evening
  GEORGINA to the theatre
7 FRANZ   to the theatre on Tuesday evening
  GEORGINA to a football match
8 FRANZ   to a concert on Thursday evening
  GEORGINA to a party

D   Study this conversation:

KURT   Would you like to come to the cinema this
          evening?
GEORGINA I'd rather go for a walk, I think.

Continue in the same way:

1 KURT   to the theatre   4 KURT   for a walk
  GEORGINA for a walk   GEORGINA to the football match
2 KURT   to the cinema   5 KURT   to the party
  GEORGINA to a concert   GEORGINA for a walk
3 KURT   to the football match   6 KURT   to the cinema
  GEORGINA to the cinema   GEORGINA to the party

READING COMPREHENSION

Rolf is German. He is on holiday in London. His friend
Beatriz lives in Spain.

10 July

The Queen's Hotel,
Buckingham Palace Road,
London SW1.

Dear Beatriz,
   Thank you for your postcard. Do you like my address?
Unfortunately 'she' doesn't live at our end of the street'.
You are right about the English food. The English eat too many
potatoes and the coffee is awful. But I like London. I like
the big, red buses and I like the policemen. I find them very
friendly and helpful.
   This afternoon we are going to Windsor. Write soon.
        Love, Rolf.

P.S. SOME NEW STAMPS ARE COMING OUT NEXT WEEK. WOULD YOU
LIKE ME TO SEND YOU SOME?

E Questions

1 Ask if Rolf likes London.
2 Answer the question.
3 Who is 'She'?
4 What does Rolf think of English coffee?
5 What does he say about potatoes?
6 Ask if Rolf likes English policemen.
7 Answer the question.
8 Why?
9 Where is Rolf going in the afternoon?
10 What does Rolf offer to do?
11 Why do you think Rolf writes to Beatriz in English?

GRAMMAR SUMMARY

F Note *Do you like . . . ?*

and *Would you like . . . ?*

Do you like coffee?	Yes, I do. No, I don't.

Would you like	a cup of tea?	Yes, please. No, thank you.
	to come to the cinema?	Oh, that would be lovely. I'm afraid I can't.

Georgina can't go.

FRANZ   Would you like to come to the theatre this
            evening?
GEORGINA   I'm afraid I can't; I'm going to the cinema.

'I'm afraid . . .' is a way of saying: 'I'm sorry . . .'

'I'm going . . .' is an example of the **present continuous**
tense used as a future.

I'm (I am) You're (you are) He's, she's (he is, she is) We're (we are) You're (you are) They're (they are)	*going*	to the cinema to a party to a concert	this evening. tomorrow. on Saturday.

In the next unit we shall practise using the **present
continuous** for an action that is taking place while we
are speaking.

Note how we use *I'd rather . . .*

'Would you like to come for a walk?'
'*I'd rather* go to the disco.'

LISTENING ACTIVITIES

G   Listen to these people talking about things they like, things they don't like and things they sometimes like. Kurt is talking to Georgina.

Listen again to the conversation and listen carefully to the question. Then put a tick in the correct box.

yes	no	sometimes	don't know

Now listen to the next example and do the same.

yes	no	sometimes	don't know

Here are more conversations. Listen and tick the correct boxes.

	yes	no	sometimes	don't know
A				
B				
C				
D				
E				
F				
G				
H				

H   Study these two dialogues:

'Do you like coffee?'
'Yes, I do (*or* No, I don't) (*or* Not very much).'

'Would you like a cup of coffee?'
'Yes, please (*or* No, thank you).'

Now reply to the following questions:

1 Do you like chocolate?
2 Would you like a piece of chocolate?
3 Would you like a cigarette?
4 Do you like real coffee?
5 Would you like a cup of coffee?
6 Do you like pop music?
7 Do you like ice cream?
8 Would you like an ice cream?
9 Would you like another cup of coffee?
10 Do you like grapes?

I   Sometimes we don't want to reply *yes* or *no* to questions like this.

Study these dialogues:

Would you like to watch television?
It depends what's on.

Do you like pop music?
It depends what sort of pop music, or *It depends on* the group.

*Reply to the following questions, using **it depends . . .** or **it depends on . . .***

1 Would you like to come to the cinema?
2 Do you like music?
3 Would you like to come to a football match tomorrow?
4 Do you like cheese?
5 Are you going to the seaside tomorrow?
6 Do you like coffee?

J   You meet Sally at a party. You want to know if she likes pop music. You say:

'Do you like pop music?'

Now you want to invite her to have some orange juice. You say:

'Would you like some orange juice?'

Now ask more questions:

 1 You want to know if she likes dancing.
 2 You want to invite her to have a sandwich.
 3 You want to invite her to have some more orange juice.
 4 You want to know if she likes pop music.
 5 You want to know if she likes watching television.
 6 You want to invite her to have another sandwich.
 7 You want to invite her to have a piece of cake.
 8 You want to know if she likes classical music.
 9 You want to know if she likes her job.
10 You want to invite her to dance.

HOMEWORK EXERCISES

A

1 You want to invite a friend to come with you to the theatre tomorrow evening. What do you say?
2 A friend invites you to go to a football match. You don't want to go. Say 'no' politely.
3 A friend invites you to go to a party on Friday evening. Accept.
4 Invite a friend to have a cup of coffee.
5 Ask a friend if he likes marmalade.

B   Reply to the following questions:

1 Do you like coffee?
2 Do you like watching television?
3 Would you like some coffee?
4 Would you like a piece of chocolate cake?
5 Do you like football?

C   Look at this conversation:

'What are you doing this evening?'
'I'm meeting Sarah.'

Answer the following questions using 'I'm . . . ing'.

1 What are you doing tomorrow?
2 What are you doing on Saturday?
3 What are you doing on Sunday?
4 Where are you going for your holiday?

D   Dictation

This evening I am going to the cinema. I sometimes go with Beatriz, but this evening I am going alone. Beatriz is nice, but she talks a lot and when I go to the cinema I like to watch the film.

   The film I am going to is an old one, but it is very good. It is a Hitchcock film.

STUDY THE WORDS

Remember these words (look at the Dialogue):

Going out:

afternoon	cinema
evening	party
invitation	ballet
football match	theatre

A person can be:
friendly   helpful   right

Other words in this unit (can you find them?):

address	lovely	unfortunately
policeman	soon	

Can you tell me the way?

DIALOGUE

Pete is standing outside the station.

PETE   Excuse me. Can you tell me the best way to get to the Bridge Hotel?

MAN   Yes. Go straight down Midland Road till you come to the traffic lights. Turn right into the High Street, cross the Town bridge and you'll find the Bridge Hotel on the right.

PETE   Thanks.

A   Questions

1 Where is Pete standing?
2 What is he looking for?
3 What must he cross?
4 Is the hotel on the left or the right?

B   Pete wants to know where the theatre is. He says:

'Can you tell me where the theatre is?'

Look at the map. The answer is:

'It's in Midland Road, near the station.'

Practise the conversation

1 —— the cinema?
2 —— the Bridge Hotel?
3 —— the police station?
4 —— the library?
5 —— the football ground?
6 —— St Mary's Church?
7 —— the hospital?
8 —— the Swan Hotel?
9 —— the bookshop?
10 —— the museum?

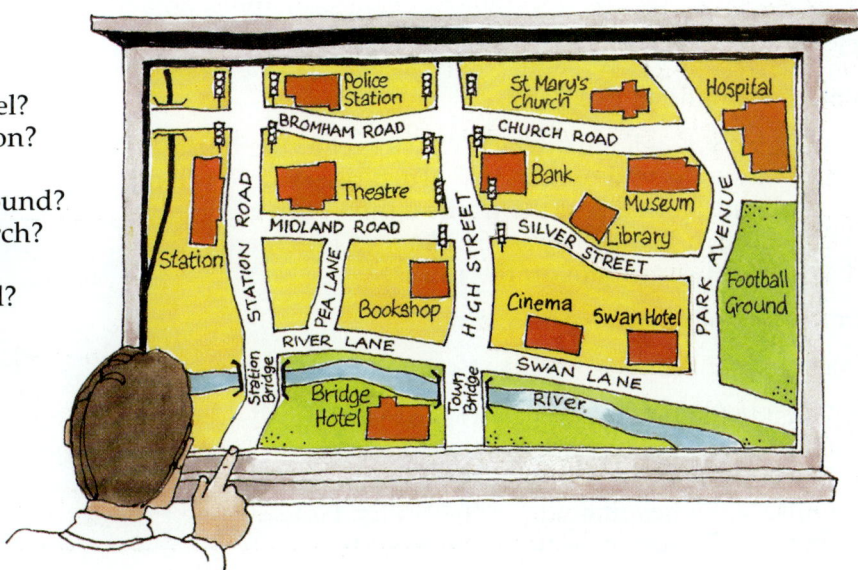

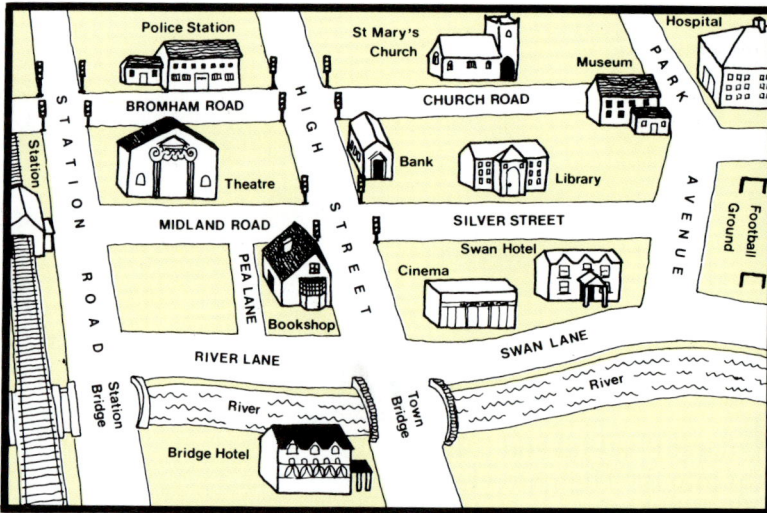

C   Look at this conversation:

Pete is standing outside the bookshop in the High Street.

PETE   Excuse me, I'm looking for the police station.

MAN   Go straight down the High Street till you come to the
2nd traffic lights. Turn left into Bromham Road and
you'll see the police station on the right.

Practise asking for and giving directions.

You are standing:	You want to get to:
1 Outside the theatre	the bookshop
2 Outside the bookshop	St Mary's Church
3 Outside the museum	the bookshop
4 Outside the theatre	the library
5 Outside the police station	the bank

D   Here is a more complicated situation.

Pete is standing in Pea Lane.

PETE   Can you tell me the best way to get to the museum?

MAN   Go to the end of this road. Turn right into Midland
Road. Turn left at the traffic lights. Turn right into
Church Road. Go past St Mary's Church and you'll
find the museum on the right.

Practise asking and giving directions.

You are standing:	You want to get to:
1 Outside the theatre	the Swan Hotel
2 Outside the police station	the cinema
3 Outside the station	the football ground
4 Outside the hospital	the Bridge Hotel
5 Outside the station	the hospital

E   Sometimes you need information about longer journeys. Then you visit a travel agency.

Destination	Single £	Return £
Athens	68	100
Buenos Aires	460	700
Barcelona	79	112
Caracas	390	550
Lima	420	640
Milan	69	97
Mexico City	380	530
New York	89	163
Rio de Janeiro	410	650
Sao Paulo	425	660
Tokyo	335	570
Zurich	67	91

PETE   Good morning. I want to book a flight to Caracas next weekend. Can you tell me how much it costs?

TRAVEL AGENT   Single or return?

PETE   Return please.

TRAVEL AGENT   £550

PETE   Thank you.

Look at the list of prices and destinations and practise similar conversations.

LISTENING ACTIVITIES

F   It is Saturday afternoon. Pete is in Timpsford. He is looking for the football ground so he asks a man in the street.

Listen to the conversation.

1   Now answer this question:

Where in Timpsford are Pete and the man?
Listen again and look at the map on page 50. You have two minutes. Do you know the answer? Does your neighbour know the answer? Listen again and check your answer with your teacher.

2   Now look at the next listening activity.

You will have to listen and write some words. You know all the words.

PETE   Excuse me _____ you tell me _____ the football ground is?

MAN   Yes, of course. _____ you got a _____ ?

PETE   Sorry. I'm _____ I haven't.

MAN   Well, let me see. Turn _____ and go _____ the bridge. Then turn _____ into Silver Street. Walk to the end of Silver Street. You'll find the football ground _____ _____ _____ you. You can't miss it.

PETE   (*repeats, as before.*) Turn left. Turn right. Walk to the end of the street.

Check answers with your neighbours and teacher.

3 Here is the last listening activity.

Listen again and write the words you can hear but can't see.
Remember, Pete hasn't got a map, but the man has one.

MAN   Look here. I've got a map of Timpsford. _____
        you like _____ ?

PETE   Yes, please, I understand maps _____ _____
        English.

READING COMPREHENSION

Rosario Hotel, Ibiza.
17th August.

Dear Pat,
    I hope you and Kathy are well and that Mr. Fox is not giving you too many letters to type.
    We're being very lazy and enjoying the Spanish sunshine. It's very hot. I'm sitting beside the swimming pool now, with a cool glass of lemonade beside me — just like the television advertisements.
    Don has his movie camera with him. He says he is making a great holiday movie. This gives him a good excuse for looking at all the pretty girls.
    I must stop now. It's lunch-time. Remember me to everybody.

Love, Louise.

G   Read Louise's letter and put a ✓

	Yes	No
Examples: Pat is on holiday.		✓
Louise is on holiday.	✓	
1 Louise is in Spain.		
2 Pat types letters.		
3 Louise has her movie camera with her.		
4 Louise is sitting beside the sea.		
5 Louise is drinking warm lemonade.		
6 Don is making a holiday movie.		
7 The weather is hot and sunny.		
8 Louise is being very lazy.		

GRAMMAR SUMMARY

H   Study these ideas:

. . . I'm looking for an underground station.
. . . we are . . . enjoying the Spanish sunshine.
I'm sitting beside the swimming pool . . .
You are making too much noise.

In each of these ideas the verb is in the **present continuous**
tense. In unit eight we noted that this tense is often used
with a time word to describe a future action. In the examples
above it is used to describe something that is taking place
while the speaker is speaking.

Statements

I'm (I am) You're (you are) He's, she's (he is, she is) We're (we are) You're (you are) They're (they are)	*making*	too much noise.

Questions

Am I Are you Is he, is she Are we Are you Are they	*making*	too much noise?

Negatives

I'm not (I am not) You aren't (you are not) He isn't, she isn't (He is not, she is not) We aren't (we are not) You aren't (you are not) They aren't (they are not)	*making*	too much noise.

I Look at the pictures and say what the people are doing.

1 walk

2 eat

3 run

4 watch

5 dance

6 play (tennis)

7 take

8 swim

9 drive

10 ride

11 come (out of)

12 wait for

13 go to

14 listen to

HOMEWORK EXERCISES

A Look again at the map of Timpsford on page 50.

1 Mr Ashley is at the Bridge Hotel. He says to you: 'Excuse me, can you tell me the best way to get to the museum?'

Answer the question.

2 Tom is at the railway station. He says to you: 'Excuse me, can you tell me the best way to get to the hospital?'

Answer the question.

3 You are standing outside the library when a lady comes up to you and says: 'Excuse me, I'm looking for the police station.'

What do you say?

B 1 You are in the booking office at Paddington station, London. You want to buy a ticket to Oxford and you are coming back the same day.
What do you ask for?

2 You are in a travel agency in London. You want to buy a ticket to fly to Geneva, but you will return by car with a friend.
What do you say?

3 You are in a travel agency in London. You want to know how much it will cost to go by air from London to your home country.
What do you ask?

4 You are in a travel agency in London. You want to go to York, but you don't know how to get there.
What do you ask?

C Dictation

> 16 Rose Street,
> Timpsford,
> 15th April.
>
> Dear Peter,
>   Thank you for your letter. Come and see us soon.
>   Our new flat is small, but it is in a pleasant road, near the river.
> When you come out of the station, walk straight down Midland Road,
> turn right at the traffic lights, turn left before you come to the bridge
> and go straight down Swan Lane, past the football ground. Our street,
> Rose Street, is the first turning on the left.
>
>   Love, Louise.

STUDY THE WORDS

Remember these words (look at the Dialogue):

Places:
library
police station
football ground
hospital
church
swimming pool

Other words in this unit (can you find them?):

traffic lights	cool
movie camera	lazy
lunch	pleasant
advertisement	pretty
excuse	straight

Do you know where I can get one?

John is in a ticket agency.

JOHN	Excuse me, have you got a ticket for *Romeo and Juliet?*
ASSISTANT	I'm afraid not. There aren't any left.
JOHN	I see. Do you know where I can get one?
ASSISTANT	Well, you can usually get one at the theatre.
JOHN	Thank you. Can you tell me where the theatre is?
ASSISTANT	Yes, of course. Have you got a map?

A Questions

1 Where is John?
2 Why is he there?
3 Has the assistant got a ticket?
4 What exactly does John ask?
5 What exactly does the assistant answer?
6 Is the assistant helpful?
7 Does John know where the theatre is?

B Here are five different kinds of shop:

a chemist's, a record shop, a ticket agency,
a newsagent's, a post office.

Look at this idea:

You can buy a blank cassette at a record shop.

Make more sentences.

1	a newspaper	6	some medicine
2	some aspirins	7	a theatre ticket
3	some cigarettes	8	a magazine
4	a record	9	some tissues
5	a stamp	10	some sweets

C Look at these conversations:

JOHN   Do you know where I can get a ticket for
        My Fair Lady?
FRIEND You can usually get one at the theatre.
JOHN   Do you know how much it will cost?
FRIEND It depends.

JOHN   Do you know where I can get some cigarettes?
FRIEND You can usually get them at a newsagent's.
JOHN   Do you know how much they will cost?
FRIEND It depends.

Complete the following conversations in the same way:

1 Do you know where I can get a newspaper?
2 Do you know where I can get some sweets?
3 Do you know where I can get a film for this camera?
4 Do you know where I can get a stamp?
5 Do you know where I can get some tissues?
6 Do you know where I can get a blank cassette?
7 Do you know where I can get some aspirins?
8 Do you know where I can get a pen?

D Learn how to tell the time in English. Then cover up the answers and practise.

JOHN   Excuse me. Can you tell me the time?
ANSWER It's exactly/about one o'clock.

It's one o'clock

It's one forty-five
(It's a quarter to two)

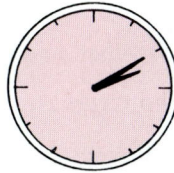

It's two ten
(It's ten past two)

It's two thirty-five
(It's twenty-five to three)

It's one fifteen
(It's a quarter past one)

It's two o'clock

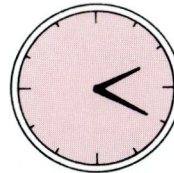

It's two twenty
(It's twenty past two)

It's two forty
(It's twenty to three)

It's one thirty
(It's half past one)

It's two-o-five
(It's five past two)

It's two twenty-five
(It's twenty-five past two)

It's two fifty
(It's ten to three)

57

E John wants to know what time the football match starts.

JOHN   Do you know what time the football match starts?
PETER   Yes, it starts at 7.30.

Talk about what's on.

WHAT'S ON THIS WEEK

FILMS

ODEON CINEMA
Monday–Saturday
ZULU
Two performances 5pm 8pm

ABC CINEMA
Monday–Saturday
LOVE STORY
Two performances 5.30pm 8.30pm
Special children's show: Saturday

PLAZA CINEMA
Monday–Saturday
STREETS OF NEW YORK
Two performances 6pm 9pm

SPORT

FOOTBALL
Eagles v Forest United
Saturday, 6th December
Town Ground, Kick-off 3pm

THEATRE

ROYAL THEATRE
Monday–Saturday
Frank Devonshire, Christine Victoria,
Sidney Allen in
COMING HOME
8pm nightly

MUSIC – ROCK, JAZZ CONCERTS

RIVERSIDE STOMPERS
George and Dragon 8pm
Monday, 1st December

ROCKY CLARKE BAND
George and Dragon 7.30pm
Wednesday, 3rd December

IAN MACKENZIE BLUES BAND
Eagle Tavern 8pm
Friday, 5th December

MUSIC – CLASSICAL

Organ Recital by John Bird
St Mary's Church
11.30am Monday, 1st December
(Entrance free)

Bach Concert
University Theatre
8pm Friday, 5th December

LISTENING ACTIVITIES

F Look at the advertisement of *What's on this week.*

Listen to the conversations. Put a circle round the correct answer.
Like this:

Yes	No

Now listen to more conversations and do the same.

1	Yes	No
2	Yes	No
3	Yes	No
4	Yes	No
5	Yes	No
6	Yes	No

G   Look at the chart below and make more conversations.

Do you know what time	the performance the film the concert the football match	starts? finishes?
	the cinema the theatre the bank the record shop	opens? closes?

Examples:

Do you know what time the film *Zulu* starts?
Yes, the second performance starts at 8 pm.

Do you know what time it finishes?
About 10.30, I think.

READING COMPREHENSION

Susie comes from Switzerland. She works in a travel agency
in Zurich. A lot of tourists visit the travel agency where she
works and she answers their questions.

   Mr and Mrs Martinez are in the travel agency at the
moment. Their home is in Caracas and they are spending
three months travelling around Europe. They want to fly
from Zurich to Madrid. They want to know the name of a
good hotel.

   They want a double room with a shower. They want to
change some money so that they can buy some presents and
they want to know where the post office is because they
have to buy some stamps. They need the stamps because
they want to send some postcards home to Venezuela.

H   Questions

1 Is Susie Swiss?
2 Does she work in a travel agency?
3 Is Mr Martinez married?
4 Is Mrs Martinez in Madrid?
5 Where does she come from?
6 Where does Mr Martinez want to go?
7 How do Mr and Mrs Martinez want to travel
    to Madrid?
8 What sort of hotel do they want?
9 What sort of room do they want?
10 Why do they want to change some money?
11 Why do they want to find a post office?
12 Why do they need stamps?

GRAMMAR SUMMARY

I Study these ideas:

Can you tell me where the theatre is?
Do you know where I can get one?
You can usually get one at the theatre.

Can and the negative form *can't* are very useful.

Statements

I You He/she We You They	*can*	get tickets at the theatre.

Questions

Can	I you he/she we you they	get tickets at the theatre?

Negatives

I You He/she We You They	*can't*	get tickets at the theatre, there aren't any left.

Note: want

Statements

I You	want	a room at the hotel.
He/she	wants	
We You They	want	to fly to Madrid.

Questions

Do you		a room at the hotel?
Does he/ she	want	to fly to Madrid?
Do you/ they		

Negatives

I You	don't		a room at the hotel.
He/she	doesn't	want	to fly to Paris.
We You They	don't		

Notice also the useful question form:

Do you know	where I can get a ticket? what time the performance starts? how much it costs?

J   Mr and Mrs Martinez live in Caracas.
Mr Martinez says: 'We live in Caracas.'

Here is some more information about Mr and Mrs Martinez. What does Mr Martinez say?

1 Mr and Mrs Martinez are spending three months in Europe.
2 Mr and Mrs Martinez want to fly to Madrid.
3 Mr and Mrs Martinez want to know the name of a good hotel.
4 Mr and Mrs Martinez don't want to pay too much for their hotel.
5 Mr and Mrs Martinez want a double room with a shower.
6 Mr and Mrs Martinez want to change some money.
7 Mr and Mrs Martinez need the money to buy some presents.
8 Mr and Mrs Martinez are looking for a post office.
9 Mr and Mrs Martinez want to buy some stamps.
10 Mr and Mrs Martinez need the stamps because they want to send some postcards home to Venezuela.

HOMEWORK EXERCISES

A   You want to ask where you can get a ticket for the football match.
What do you say? Then you ask how much it will cost.

Example: 'Can you tell me where I can get a ticket for the football match?'

'Thank you and can you tell me how much it will cost?'

1 You want to ask politely where you can get a film for your camera. What do you say? Then you ask how much it will cost.

2 A friend wants to know where he can get a birthday card. What do you say to him?

3 You are in a ticket agency. You want to know if they've got two tickets for *Chicago* for tonight. What do you say? Then you ask how much they will cost.

4 Ask a friend what time the bank opens.

5 You want to know where to get a new, and rather special pop record. Ask a friend who has it. Then you ask how much it will cost.

B Make negatives:

Example: I like milk.
I don't like milk.

1 I want an expensive room.
2 I can see the castle.
3 John can get tickets for the concert tonight.
4 I know what time the concert starts.
5 Peter wants to go home.

C What's the time?

1  3  5

2  4

D Dictation

Good afternoon, my name is Schwartz. That is
S–C–H–W–A–R–T–Z and I come from New York. My wife
and I would like a double room with a shower. I have our
passports here. We are hoping to stay for about a week. I
have a question. Do you know where I can get two tickets
for the performance at the theatre tonight?

STUDY THE WORDS

Study these words (look at the Dialogue and the Reading comprehension):

In the shop:
assistant
cigarettes
birthday card
tissues
sweets
blank cassette
present
stamp
newsagent's
chemist's
post office

A show:
show
performance
organ
concert
ticket agency

Other words in this unit (can you find them?):
medicine
tourists
stamp
passport
shower

Here is your second progress test. You can use a lot of English now so this test is more difficult.

1 Remember David. He lives *in* a flat *near* Victoria Station. Now look at the example.

David lives _____ a flat _____ Victoria Station.

Write the missing words. Look at the illustration of David's flat and write the missing words again. Use: *in, between, on, under, near, at, behind, in front of, above.*

1 The television is _____ the window.
2 There are a lot of books _____ the shelves.
3 The shelves are _____ the television.
4 There is a chair _____ the television and the window.
5 There is a big envelope _____ the clock.
6 The clock is _____ the big envelope.
7 The table is _____ the window.

Now write about David.

8 David cooks his food _____ the kitchen.
9 David lives _____ his office.
10 David eats his dinner _____ the table.

2 Read this story about Helen and Sue. They live in the same flat. Helen often borrows Sue's clothes and she doesn't always ask. Sue gets angry when she can't find things.

Now, answer these statements with **Yes** or **No**.

	Yes	No
1 Helen and Sue have the same address.		
2 Sue often lends her clothes to Helen.		
3 Sue is happy when Helen borrows her clothes.		

3 Now look at the conversation between Helen and Sue.
Think. Try to complete the conversation.

SUE   Helen, I'm looking for _____ blue sweater. Have
           you got it?

HELEN   No, I _____ .

SUE   Are you sure? I think that sweater is _____ .

HELEN   No, it isn't yours. It _____ to me.

SUE   It looks like _____ .

HELEN   You always say that. Is this flat yours?

SUE   No, it's _____ and _____ .

4 Look at this example:

KURT   Would you like an ice cream, Georgina?

GEORGINA   Sorry, I *never* eat ice cream.

Now use the words: *never, always, usually, sometimes,* and
often to complete these sentences.

  1 Maria has a day off every Sunday. She _____ works on
     Sunday.

  2 Maria works five days every week. She walks to work
     four days a week. She _____ walks to work.

  3 Maria goes shopping every Saturday.
     She _____ goes shopping on Saturday.

  4 Georgina likes good coffee.
     She can't find good coffee very often.
     She _____ drinks good coffee.

  5 Maria likes sweet things. She _____ eats sweet things.

5 Here is a short story about Sally and Frank:

Sally is 20. She has a fast car and an expensive flat. Frank
is 42. He has an old car and a cheap flat. Sally wants to
marry Frank. Frank wants to marry Sally. What are the
problems?

  1 Frank is _____ than Sally. Sally is _____ than Frank.

  2 Sally's flat is _____ _____ than Frank's.

  3 Frank's flat is cheaper _____ Sally's.

  4 Sally's car is _____ _____ Frank's.

  5 Frank's car is _____ _____ Sally's.

6 Talk to your neighbours about Sally and Frank.

  1 Do you think the difference in age is important?

  2 Do you think the difference in money is important?

Where did you go yesterday?

DIALOGUE

JOANNA	Where did you go yesterday?
FRANK	I went to Croydon.
JOANNA	Did you go shopping?
FRANK	No, I went for an interview.
JOANNA	Oh, did you get a job?
FRANK	Yes, I got a job as a Management Trainee.
JOANNA	Fantastic.

A   Read the Dialogue and put a ✓

	Yes	No
Example: Frank went shopping.		✓
Frank went to Croydon.	✓	
1 Frank went to Croydon yesterday.		
2 Joanna went for an interview.		
3 Joanna got a job.		
4 Frank went for an interview.		
5 Frank got a job.		
6 Joanna is pleased.		

B   Read the story.

Frank wanted a job, so last week he bought a newspaper and looked at the advertisements. He saw this one:

> **WANTED. MANAGEMENT TRAINEES FOR BIG STORE. RING 553 4443**

He phoned the number in the advertisement and spoke to the Personnel Manager, Mr Allen. Mr Allen asked Frank to visit him at three o'clock that afternoon.

Frank wore his blue suit for the interview. He looked very smart. Mr Allen asked Frank a lot of questions. Then he said:
'All right Frank, you can start on Monday.'

*Read the story again carefully and underline the **verbs.** They are not new. But some of them are in the **simple past tense** because these things happened last week.*

C   Answer these questions about the story:

Example: What did Frank want?
          A job.

1 What did Frank want?
2 What did he buy?
3 What did he look at?
4 What did he see?
5 Which number did he phone?
6 Who did he speak to?
7 What did Mr Allen ask Frank to do?
8 What did Frank wear for the interview?
9 Did he look smart?
10 How many questions did Mr Allen ask Frank?

D   Now talk about things that happened to you. Use complete sentences.

Example: Talk about somewhere you went last year.
          I went to Paris last year.

1 Talk about somebody you spoke to yesterday.
2 Talk about something you bought last week.
3 Talk about something you ate yesterday.
4 Talk about something you heard on the radio.
5 Talk about somebody you saw yesterday.
6 Talk about what you wore last Sunday.
7 Talk about somewhere you went last Saturday.
8 Talk about something you enjoyed last week.
9 Talk about something you gave one of your family as a present.
10 Talk about a place you visited last week.

READING COMPREHENSION

Enrico rang the bell and his landlady opened the door. 'Did you forget your key?' she asked.
   'I'm sorry,' he said, 'I lost it.'   I've lost it.
   'Oh, no. Where did you lose it?'
   'I don't know. I had it yesterday.'
   'I haven't got another one for you.'
   'I'm sorry,' he said again.
   She disappeared into the kitchen and he went upstairs to his room. He took off his jacket and trousers and put on his old blue jeans. As he did so he felt something hard in the back pocket. It was the key.

E   Questions

1 Who opened the door?
2 Did Enrico forget his key?
3 What did Enrico do with his key?
4 Does Enrico know where he lost it?
5 How does Enrico apologise? ('He says . . .')
6 Where did Enrico's landlady go after their conversation?
7 Where did Enrico go?
8 What did Enrico take off?
9 What did he put on?
10 Where did he find the key?

GRAMMAR SUMMARY

F   The **simple past** tense is the tense we use when we are telling a story. In English we use the **simple past** for anything that happened *at a special point of time* in the past. Sometimes the point of time is understood.

Where did you go yesterday?
I went for an interview. (yesterday)
I got a job . . . (yesterday)
. . . last week he bought a newspaper . . .

These regular verbs end in –*ed*. They look the same, but they sound different.

sound:	-d	-t	-id
	apologise — apologised arrive — arrived answer — answered live — lived	ask — asked finish — finished like — liked look — looked talk — talked walk — walked work — worked	visit — visited want — wanted wait — waited

However there are many irregular verbs.
Here are the past forms of some you already know:

buy — bought
can — could
come — came
eat — ate
find — found
forget — forgot
feel — felt

know — knew
leave — left
lose — lost
put — put
ring — rang
run — ran
see — saw

give — gave
go — went
get — got
have — had
hear — heard
keep — kept

sell — sold
sit — sat
spend — spent
take — took
tell — told
wear — wore

Statements

I You He/she We You They	saw bought got	a newspaper this morning.

Questions

Note this form carefully:

Did	you he/she we you they	see buy get	a newspaper this morning?

To be is different.

Statements

I was You were He/she was We were You were They were	pleased about it.

Questions

Were you Was he/she Were we Were you Were they	pleased about it?

Note how we ask questions with: **where, when, what, why, how**

Examples: Your friend recently bought a very interesting old sports car.

When did you buy it?
Why didn't you buy a new one?
Where did you buy it?
What did you do with your other car?
How did you find this one?

G Change the verbs into the *simple past*.

Example: Enrico's landlady (open) the door.
        Enrico's landlady *opened* the door.

1 Enrico (ring) the bell.
2 He (apologise) to his landlady.
3 He (lose) his key.
4 His landlady (go) into the kitchen.
5 Enrico (take off) his jacket and trousers.
6 He (put on) his blue jeans.
7 He (feel) something hard in his pocket.
8 He (find) the key.

H Ask Enrico some questions using *did*.

Example: Ask where Enrico went.
         Where *did* you go?

1 Ask how Enrico came home.
2 Ask why Enrico rang the bell.
3 Ask where Enrico lost the key.
4 Ask how Enrico lost it.
5 Ask how Enrico found it.
6 Ask where Enrico found it.

LISTENING ACTIVITY

TO THE TOP IN FIVE YEARS

I Look at the two girls.

Are they the same girls? Which one do you think is older? Which one do you think has got more money? Which one is happier? Well, the girl at the top is Regine and the girl at the bottom is Regine, too. What is the difference?

Listen.

1 Listen to Regine again and write the missing words.

I _____ in a good department store. I _____ so much that I _____ (a) good commission. I _____ _____ the shop every morning. I lived _____ _____ . I _____ my money. I _____ _____ evening classes. I really _____ _____ _____ a success.

2 Listen to the example question and answer. Follow the instructions. You hear: 'Does Regine like her job?' Look at the answers.

Example question:

Does Regine like her job?

Example answer:

1 Yes, she does.
2 Yes, she is.
3 No, she doesn't.

Question 1
1 Yes, she does.
2 No, she didn't.
3 Yes, she did.

Question 2
1 No, she isn't.
2 No, she didn't.
3 Yes, she did.

Question 3
1 No, she doesn't.
2 Yes, she is.
3 Yes, she does.

Question 4
1 Yes, she is.
2 No, she isn't.
3 Yes, she does.

Question 5
1 No, she isn't.
2 No, she doesn't.
3 Yes, she is.

HOMEWORK EXERCISES

A   Put the verbs in brackets into the *simple past*.

It (be) very late when we (come) out of the cinema. We (know) that the last train (leave) at 11.15, so we (run) as fast as we (can) to the station. It (be) just after 11.15 when we (arrive) at the station, but the trains often leave a little late and there (be) a train standing at platform 1, so we (get) in. We (wait) for half an hour, then we (get) out. We (find) the ticket collector and (ask) him when the train was going to leave..

   'Tomorrow morning at 6 o'clock,' he told us.

   There (be) no taxis outside the station, so we (walk) home. It (take) us nearly two hours. The next morning we (feel) very tired.

B   Dictation

On my first day in London I felt hungry, so I went into a restaurant and sat down at a table. I waited for ten minutes, but nobody came to serve me. Then I saw that there were no waiters. The customers stood in a queue and got their food themselves. That was my first experience of a self-service restaurant.

STUDY THE WORDS

Remember these words (look at the Dialogue):

Jobs:
job
interview
trainee
experience
smart

Other words in this unit (can you find them?):

shopping
waiter
self-service
queue
pair of jeans

bell
landlady
pocket
conversation

I didn't buy it

DIALOGUE

CHRISTINE	When did you buy that new necklace?
LIBBY	I didn't buy it. It was a present.
CHRISTINE	Oh, who gave it to you?
LIBBY	A friend.
CHRISTINE	Anybody I know?
LIBBY	Don't ask so many questions.

A Questions

1 Who had a new necklace?
2 Did she buy it?
3 Who gave it to her?
4 Can you tell from Libby's answer if her friend was male
   or female?
   What do you think?

B Study this conversation:

CHRISTINE   She had a new necklace.
Use the past of the verb *give*.
LIBBY   Who gave it to her?

Practise asking questions in the past beginning with 'Who'.

1 The phone rang.
   _____ answer _____
2 There isn't any cake left.
   _____ eat _____
3 They sold their car.
   _____ buy _____
4 She got her diamond ring back.
   _____ find _____
5 He couldn't find the newspaper.
   _____ have _____
6 It was a marvellous photograph.
   _____ take _____

C Christine types very well. This morning she started a new job and now Libby is asking her about it. You complete the conversation:

LIBBY	(have) a nice day?
CHRISTINE	Yes, thanks.
LIBBY	What (do)?
CHRISTINE	I (get) there at 9 o'clock and I (say) I (be) Christine Taylor. Then they (give) me some letters to type.
LIBBY	(type) them well?
CHRISTINE	Yes, of course. I (type) them as well as I could. Then at lunchtime two of the girls (take) me to a sandwich bar near the office and we (eat) some sandwiches.
LIBBY	What else (do)?
CHRISTINE	Oh, I (answer) one or two telephone calls.
LIBBY	Do you think you're going to like it there?
CHRISTINE	Oh, yes if they don't give me too many letters to type.

READING COMPREHENSION

My name is Henry. I started work at the bank the same day as Eric Lucas. He was intelligent, but he didn't work very hard. He was interested in girls, but he wasn't very interested in his job. After about two years he left.

He got a job in a supermarket and then he worked for an insurance company. After that he joined the army and went abroad, so I didn't see him for several years. Then he left the army and got a job with an American airline.

I am nearly forty now and I still work at the bank. This morning a big car stopped outside, and a beautiful American girl came into the bank and asked to change a thousand dollars in travellers' cheques. Her husband was with her. He was older than she was and at first I didn't recognise him. Then he smiled at me. It was Eric.

D Questions

1 Where does Henry work?
2 What was Eric interested in?
3 How long did he stay at the bank?
4 Where did he work after he left the bank?
5 Did Eric pay to go abroad?
6 Who paid?
7 Who did Eric work for after leaving the army?
8 Is Eric's wife younger than Eric?
9 Why did the American girl come into the bank?
10 Why did her husband smile at Henry?

Now look at the text again, and find three things that Henry didn't do and Eric did.

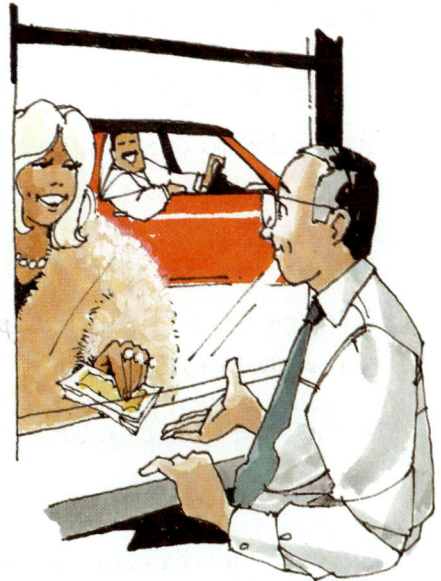

GRAMMAR SUMMARY

E   Note the negative form of the *simple past*:

I You He/she We You They	*didn't*	see buy get	a newspaper this morning.

And the negative of *to be*:

I wasn't You weren't He/she wasn't We weren't You weren't They weren't	pleased about it.

Note: I didn't see *him*.
Her husband was with *her*.
He smiled at *me*.

Here is the full list of pronouns:

She	looked at	*me* *you* *him/her/it* *us* *you* *them*

Note these questions:

Where When	did you find	it?
Who	found	

**F   Read the story about Eric Lucas again. Then imagine
you are asking Eric some questions.**

Example: Ask if Eric liked his job at the bank.
        Did you like your job at the bank?

1 Ask if he liked his job at the bank.
2 Ask if he worked hard.
3 Ask why he left the bank.
4 Ask if he worked in a supermarket.
5 Ask if he had a job with an insurance company.
6 Ask when he joined the army.
7 Ask where they sent him.
8 Ask why he went to America.
9 Ask who he met there.
10 Ask if she worked for the airline too.

G Now put the verbs in the text below into the *simple past*. To make sense you'll have to put some of them into the *negative*.

I knew Eric Lucas. He (be) stupid. He (like) girls but he (like) his job very much. He (leave) the bank after two years. He (get) a job in a newsagent's ~~then~~ he (get) a job in a supermarket. Later he (work) for an American airline. He (marry) an English girl, he (marry) a beautiful American girl. Last week Eric and his wife (visit) the bank.

H Look at this conversation.

Example: Did you sell your car?
          No, I didn't.

Now answer the questions using **didn't.**

1 Did you buy that camera?
2 Did he ask Sylvia about it?
3 Did you and your wife speak to the doctor?
4 Did George and Helen telephone the Bank Manager?
5 Did she tell George about it?
6 Did John eat the last piece of cake?
7 Did Sarah invite Roger?
8 Did you all answer the questions?

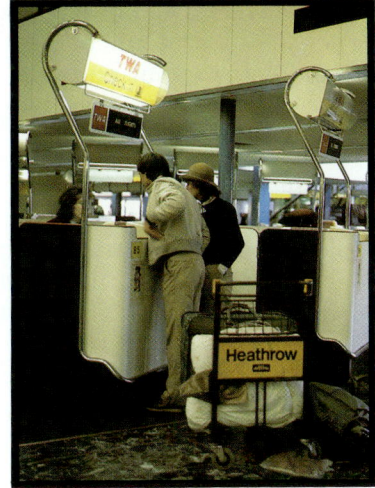

LISTENING ACTIVITIES

I Listen to the tape.

1 Now look at this sentence. Underline the true or false answer, like this:

Does Eric work in a bank?
No, of course he doesn't.   So you underline *False.*

Example:
Eric works in a bank.   True   <u>False</u>

Go on with more sentences:

	True	False
1 Henry speaks to Eric first.	True	False
2 Henry is pleased to see Eric.	True	False
3 Eric is married.	True	False
4 Eric wanted to change some travellers' cheques.	True	False
5 It is almost lunch-time.	True	False

2 Now listen again to Henry, Eric and Marina, Eric's wife. They are having lunch. *Before* you listen look at the statements in your book.
Say whether these statements are true or false like the others.

1 Eric and Henry didn't start work on the same day.	True	False	
2 Henry's birthday is on the third of April.	True	False
3 Henry started work at thirty.	True	False
4 Henry is younger than forty.	True	False
5 Marina thinks Henry looks old.	True	False

The conversation continues. Listen to it.

3 Listen to the conversation again and write all the numbers you hear, in figures.
Here is an example:
  Listen to Henry and Eric.
  Did you hear the number 22?
  Write the number in box 1.
  Now listen and write the other numbers.

1 ☐   3 ☐   5 ☐   7 ☐   9 ☐

2 ☐   4 ☐   6 ☐   8 ☐

4 Can you answer some problem questions? Here is the first:
  Henry, Eric and Marina are having lunch on the fifteenth of April, 1981. Henry is nearly forty.
  So when was he born? In _____ .
  Eric is two years older than Henry.
  When was he born? In _____ .

Those were examples. Here are the real problems. Work with another student to answer them.
Listen to the tape.

1 When did Eric start at the bank? In _____ .
2 When did he leave the bank? In _____ .
3 When did he leave the supermarket? _____ .
4 When did he leave the army? _____ .
5 When is he going to retire? _____ .

HOMEWORK EXERCISES

A Read this story about Peter.

Peter left school when I did and he got a job in a supermarket. He stayed there for two years and then he joined the police. But he wasn't happy, so he left the police and found a job in the local bookshop. He is still there.

Now ask questions.

1 Ask when Peter left school.
2 Ask how long he stayed at the supermarket.
3 Ask what he did then.
4 Ask why he left the police.
5 Ask where he found another job.
6 Ask if he still works there.

B Study the examples. Say what Peter did or did not do.

Examples: go/university
He didn't go to university.

get a job/supermarket
He got a job in a supermarket.

1 get a job/bank
2 stay at the supermarket/for two years
3 join/the army
4 join/the police force
5 leave/the police force
6 find a job/in the local library

C· Now you are talking to Peter:

1 Ask why he got a job in the supermarket.
2 Ask why he joined the police force.
3 Ask if he wore a uniform every day.
4 Ask if he liked being a policeman.
5 Ask when he got the job at the bookshop.

D Dictation

I am not going out with George again. Last week he invited
me to go to a football match. I do not like football, so it was
silly of me to say yes. We did not have seats, so we had to
stand for two hours in the rain. I was cold and wet and I
could not see a thing. So I asked George to take me home.
He got very angry and said some very unpleasant things.

STUDY THE WORDS

Remember these words (look at the Reading comprehension):

A person can be:
intelligent
interested
angry
silly
unpleasant
stupid

Other words in this unit (can you find them?):

diamond
necklace
insurance
travellers' cheques
airline
abroad

army
beautiful
sandwich
cake
uniform
university

What are you going to do now?

ANGELA How did you get on in your exam?
BOB   I failed.
ANGELA Oh, I *am* sorry. What are you going to do now?
BOB   I'm going to take it again, of course.
ANGELA When are you going to take it?
BOB   I'm definitely not going to take it until next year.

A   Questions

1 Who took the exam?
2 Ask if he passed.
3 Answer the question.
4 What is he going to do?
5 Ask if he's going to take the exam again this year.
6 Answer the question.

B   Study this pattern:

Bob didn't pass the exam
take
so he's going to take it again.

Complete the following sentences about Bob, using **going to.**

1 There's a good play on television
   watch
2 The phone's ringing
   answer
3 There's an interesting story in the paper
   read
4 Angela is making Bob a cup of coffee
   drink
5 Bob isn't enjoying the party
   leave
6 There's a nice steak in front of Bob. He's hungry
   eat

C You are going to buy a birthday present for a friend. You can't spend more than £10. What are you going to buy?

READING COMPREHENSION

From the diary of a student called Andy.

D Read what Andy wrote in his diary and put a ✓

Example:	Yes	No
Paulette wants to go out with Andy on Sunday.		✓
1 Last week was a bad week for Andy.		
2 Andy talked to Paulette on the telephone.		
3 The bank manager wrote a letter to Andy.		
4 Andy has a lot of money in the bank.		
5 Andy hopes his Uncle Frank is going to help him.		
6 Andy got his exam results on Friday.		
7 Andy's exam marks were very good.		
8 Andy is going to work very hard.		

SUNDAY

Last week was awful. Tuesday Paulette telephoned. She doesn't want to go out with me again. On Wednesday I got the letter from the bank manager and on Friday the exam results came out. One disaster after another. What am I going to do? Well I'm not going to worry about Paulette. I'm going to forget her completely. But the money is a problem. I think I'm going to write to Uncle Frank. He helped last time.
   And most important of all, what am I going to do about the exam results? A lot of hard work, I'm afraid.

LISTENING ACTIVITIES

E

1 Look at the picture.
What kind of shop is it?
What can you buy there?
What is going to happen next week?

TRUE VALUE STORES

Sale Next Week!

£120·45 £98·95 £300·00 £250 £92·64 £72·64 £22·50 £20·00

Now listen to Bob and Angela.

Bob and Angela are talking about money, aren't they? They have some problems. Look at the picture. *True-Value* are going to sell cookers for £250.

Now listen to Bob and Angela again. Write, in figures, all the sums of money you hear.

1 Bob wants a hi-fi. It's going to cost _____ .
2 Angela wants a washing machine. It's going to cost _____ .
3 Bob and Angela can save _____ .
4 Bob thinks they have about _____ .
5 Angela is afraid they haven't got _____ .
6 Angela knows they have only _____ .

2 *Work with another student to answer these questions.*

(You can listen to Bob and Angela again. Just ask your teacher if you want to listen to them.)

1 Bob wants a hi-fi and Angela wants a washing machine. How much money are they planning to spend? _____ .
2 How much money have they got? _____ .
3 How much money are they going to need? _____ .

GRAMMAR SUMMARY

F We use the *going to* future when we want to express an intention.

What are you going to do?
I'm going to take the exam again of course.
I'm not going to take it until next year.
I'm going to have a shower.

Statements

I'm You're He's/she's We're You're They're	*going to*	have a holiday.

Negatives

I'm You're He's/she's We're You're They're	*not going to*	take the exam again.

Questions

Are you Is he/is she Are we Are you Are they	going to	take the exam again?

G   You are a new student at a big English University. There are a lot of clubs and societies you can join.

Look at the list below and tell your friends which clubs you are going to join, which you *aren't* going to join and *why*.

Example:

I'm going to join the History Society because I like local history.

I'm not going to join the tennis club because I don't like tennis.

The History Society	(They study local history.)
The Book Society	(They talk about books.)
The Poetry Society	(They read poetry.)
The Football Club	(They play football.)
The Chess Club	(They play chess.)
The Tennis Club	(They play tennis.)
The Music Club	(They listen to music.)

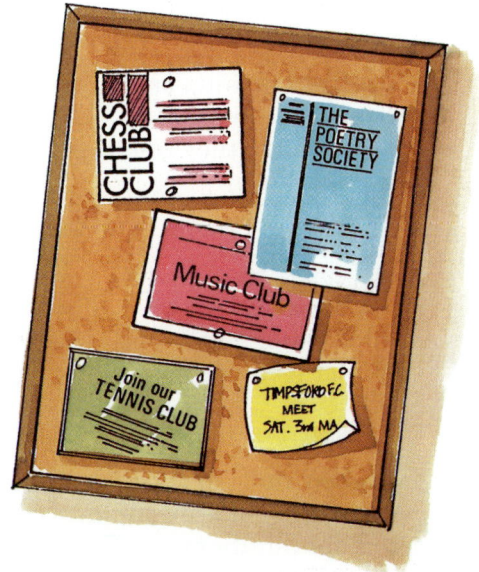

HOMEWORK EXERCISES

A   What are these people going to do?
1 John and Alice are wearing tennis clothes and they have their tennis rackets.
2 Brigitte is in the bathroom. The water is running into the bath.
3 Peter is putting a new record on the record player.
4 Tom has his camera in his hand and Alice is standing in front of an old castle. She is smiling.

B   A friend tells you he is going to buy a motor bike. Ask him questions, using *going to*?

1 _____ a new one?
2 Where _____ ?
3 What sort _____ ?
4 When _____ ?
5 How much _____ ?

UNIT 13

C Make sentences using either *going to* or *not going to*.

Example:
John could watch the news or he could watch a comedy programme on TV. He's going to watch the comedy programme, so . . .

he's not going to watch the news.

1 Peter could buy the green pullover or he could buy the blue pullover. He's going to buy the green pullover, so . . .

2 There are two good films on. Tom and Alice could see *The Orient Express*, or they could see *The Italian Job*. They're going to see *The Orient Express*, so . . .

3 Paul and Belinda are looking at the menu in a restaurant. They could have roast beef or they could have roast lamb. They decide they're not going to have roast lamb, so . . .

4 Brigitte wants to go to Edinburgh. She could travel by air or she could travel by train. She's going to travel by air, so . . .

5 The famous jockey could ride Saratoga Skiddy or he could ride Winter Fair in the big race. He's not going to ride Winter Fair, so . . .

D Dictation

Last week the sun shone and it got quite hot. I decided to put on my light grey summer trousers. But I got a shock. I could not put them on. They were too small.

It is possible that they got smaller during the winter, but I do not think so. I am afraid I got bigger. So I am going to eat less and I am going to take more exercise. I am definitely going to lose some weight.

STUDY THE WORDS

Remember these words (look at the Dialogue):

an exam
a question
a play
a story

Other words in this unit (can you find them?):

art gallery
reproduction
poetry
diary
disaster
shock

definitely
completely
the result
wrong
steak

82

It was exciting, wasn't it?

DIALOGUE

Tom and Anna saw a film yesterday.

TOM   It was exciting, wasn't it?
ANNA   Yes, it was.
TOM   Charles Bronson was good, wasn't he?
ANNA   Yes, he always is.
TOM   I thought the girl was good too.
ANNA   Did you?

A   Tom and Anna agree that Charles Bronson is a good actor. Notice another way they could say this:

TOM   I think Charles Bronson's very good.
ANNA   So do I.

If Anna disagrees, she can say: *Do you?*

Take the part of Anna and agree or disagree with the following statements:

1 I think Charlie Chaplin is very funny.
2 I like Mickey Mouse cartoons.
3 I think Marilyn Monroe is marvellous.
4 I like Tarzan films.
5 I like horror films.
6 I think there are too many Dracula films.
7 I like westerns.
8 I think Brigitte Bardot is very beautiful.

B   Look at this:

TOM   I don't like very violent films.
ANNA   Neither do I.
TOM   I didn't enjoy the film last night.
ANNA   Neither did I.

If Anna agrees, she says 'Neither do I' or 'Neither did I'.

If Anna disagrees, she uses: 'Don't you?' or 'Didn't you?'

TOM   I don't like Mickey Mouse cartoons.
ANNA   Don't you?

Take Anna's part and agree or disagree:

1 I don't like cowboy films.
2 I didn't like his last film.
3 I didn't think it was very funny.
4 I don't think he's really Mexican.
5 I didn't think she was very beautiful.
6 I didn't like the music.
7 I didn't think it was very original.
8 I don't think she's a very good actress.

C Study these conversations:

TOM   The football match was exciting, wasn't it?
ANNA   Yes, it was.

In this case Anna agrees with Tom. But look at this:

TOM   Charlie Chaplin was funny, wasn't he?
ANNA   Did you think so?

Now Anna disagrees with Tom.

Take the parts of Tom and Anna. Make a list of real films and agree or disagree about them.

Note: A film can be: exciting, funny, interesting, boring, good or awful.

READING COMPREHENSION

I think there is too much violence on television and there is too much violence in our society. There are too many war films on television, there is too much crime and there are too many murders.

There was violence in the old cowboy films of course, but in the old cowboy films there was no confusion between good and bad. The hero was very, very good and the villain was very, very bad. Now there *is* confusion. The hero is often a criminal. I think the effect on children is very bad.

There is more violent crime every year, especially in our big cities and I think there is a connection. I think that young criminals are more violent because they see so much violence on television.

D Put a ✓ against the answer the author thinks is best.

Example: There is too much violence on television.

	He thinks so	He doesn't think so	He doesn't say
	✓		

Continue in the same way

	He thinks so	He doesn't think so	He doesn't say

1 There are too many films about war on television.

2 There are too many television programmes about crime.

3 There are too many very funny programmes on television.

4 The hero in television programmes today is always very, very good.

5 There are going to be a lot more war films on television next year.

6 It's a very good thing for children to see war films on television.

7 There are some very good new television programmes coming soon.

8 Children learn a lot from watching television.

9 There is too much sport on television.

10 There is going to be more sport on television next year.

Now compare your answers with those of another student. Are they the same? Do you agree with the author? Talk about it with your neighbour.

LISTENING ACTIVITIES

E   Listen to the tape.

	Yes	No
1		
2		

Listen to the tape again.

3		
4		
5		

Dialogue 6

a Tom knows they can get a bus.
b Tom knows they can't get a bus.
c Tom isn't sure.

Dialogue 7

a Tom knows taxis are not cheap.
b Tom knows taxis are cheap.
c Tom isn't sure.

Dialogue 8

a Tom doesn't know.
b Tom has his key.
c Tom hasn't got his key.

Dialogue 9

a The money doesn't belong to Tom.
b The money could belong to Tom.
c The money belongs to Tom.

GRAMMAR SUMMARY

F In this unit you are learning how to agree and disagree with people.

Note these different ways of agreeing with someone:

So *do / did* I. and Neither *do / did* I.

Examples:

TOM	I think he's very good.
ANNA	So do I.
TOM	I don't think she's right.
ANNA	Neither do I.
TOM	I went there last week.
ANNA	So did I.
TOM	I didn't enjoy the party.
ANNA	Neither did I.

Note also:

Yes, it *is / was*. and No, it *isn't / wasn't*.

Examples:

TOM	It was funny, wasn't it?
ANNA	Yes, it was.
TOM	It isn't very interesting, is it?
ANNA	No, it isn't.

If you want to disagree, you can use:

Do you? Don't you? Didn't you? Did you think so? *or* Didn't you think so?

Examples:

TOM	I like Tarzan films.
ANNA	Do you?
TOM	I didn't think it was funny.
ANNA	Didn't you?

Note:

Is the programme going to start soon?	I hope so. I think so.
Are we late?	I hope not. I don't think so.

G   Study these conversations:

FRANK   Have you got the picnic things ready?
GWEN   Yes, but I'm afraid it's going to rain.
FRANK   I hope not.
GWEN   We're going to miss the plane.
FRANK   Don't worry. We can always get a taxi outside the station.
GWEN   I hope so.

Practise using 'I hope so' and 'I hope not'.

1 FRANK   I want to buy a birthday present.
   GWEN   I think the shops are shut this afternoon.
   FRANK   _____
2 FRANK   I want some stamps.
   GWEN   I think the post office is open till 5.30.
   FRANK   _____
3 GWEN   Why doesn't my sister write?
   FRANK   I'm sure you're going to get a letter soon.
   GWEN   _____
4 GWEN   They can repair the car, can't they?
   FRANK   Yes, but I'm afraid it's going to be expensive.
   GWEN   _____
5 GWEN   Have you got the tickets for the concert this evening?
   FRANK   No, we can get them at the door.
   GWEN   _____
6 GWEN   Anna is taking the examination next week.
   FRANK   I think she's going to pass, don't you?
   GWEN   _____

H   Frank and Gwen want to go to the cinema. They are looking at the newspaper.

FRANK   *Sunset over the prairie*?
GWEN   It's a western, isn't it?
FRANK   Yes, I think so.

Take the parts of Frank and Gwen and make more conversations.

These films are on tonight:

SWING THAT MUSIC

SUNSET OVER THE PRAIRIE

CHICAGO 1928

DANCING FEET

A LAUGH A MINUTE

WALTZING IN THE CLOUDS

OH, DOCTOR, WHAT DID YOU DO TO MY HEART?

Note:
Here are some different sorts of film: a western, a gangster film, a comedy, a musical.

HOMEWORK EXERCISES

A   You and Gwen are talking. You agree with her.

1 GWEN   It was a good film, wasn't it?
   YOU   _____
2 GWEN   I think Frank is very funny.
   YOU   _____
3 GWEN   I don't like that colour.
   YOU   _____
4 GWEN   I think it's going to be a good game.
   YOU   _____
5 GWEN   I didn't like George's friend.
   YOU   _____

B   Now disagree with Tom politely.

1 TOM   It was a good film, wasn't it?
YOU   _____
2 TOM   My goodness, these clothes are expensive.
YOU   _____
3 TOM   I think it's going to rain.
YOU   _____
4 TOM   I didn't like the play on TV last night.
YOU   _____
5 TOM   I don't like this coffee.
YOU   _____

C   Now reply to Gwen, using 'I hope so' or 'I hope not'.

1 GWEN   I'm sure it's going to rain again.
YOU   _____
2 GWEN   It's going to be a very boring evening.
YOU   _____
3 GWEN   Don't worry. The shops stay open till 5.30.
YOU   _____
4 GWEN   I'm afraid we're going to be late.
YOU   _____
5 GWEN   We can get tickets at the theatre.
YOU   _____

D   Dictation

Everything changes. Once a lot of people went to the cinema to see silent films. Then when talking pictures started nobody wanted to see silent films any more. But people still went to the cinema and everybody knew the names of all the great film stars.

Now we have television. People sit at home night after night watching their favourite programmes. But what is going to happen to the cinema?

STUDY THE WORDS

Remember these words (look at the Dialogue):

Films:
actor   violence
actress   murder
hero   confusion
villain   effect
criminal   cowboy
crime   cartoon

Films can be:
exciting   boring   silent
violent   awful
original   interesting

Other words in this unit (can you find them?):

especially   connection
picnic   marvellous
society   clever
city   favourite

I'm afraid I've had an accident

DIALOGUE

JURG	Mrs Scott . . .
MRS SCOTT	Yes?
JURG	I'm afraid I've had an accident.
MRS SCOTT	Oh, dear, what's happened?
JURG	I've spilt my coffee.
MRS SCOTT	Never mind, here's a cloth . . .

A   Questions

1 Who do you think Mrs Scott is?
2 What happened to Jurg?
3 What has Mrs Scott given him?
4 Does Mrs Scott feel angry?

B   You are in a big shop. You want to buy something, but you have forgotten your banker's card. You say:

'Good morning. I wonder if you can help me. I've forgotten my banker's card.'

What would you say in the following situations?

1 You are speaking to the bank clerk. You have lost your cheque book.
2 You left some shoes for repair. You are in the shop. You have forgotten your receipt.
3 You are speaking to the doorman at a big hotel. You were invited to a reception, but you have forgotten your invitation.
4 You are in the optician's. You have broken your glasses.
5 You are in the library. You want a book. You have lost your ticket.
6 You are talking to the doorman at the cinema. You have just come out. You have left your handbag inside.

C   Study this pattern:

'I've lost my passport.'
reported / to the police?

'Have you reported it to the police?'

Continue in the same way:

1 I've lost my key.
   looked / all your pockets?
2 I've broken a tooth.
   seen / dentist?
3 I've lost George's address.
   looked / address book?
4 I haven't found that purse I lost.
   asked / the police station?
5 I've forgotten to get any milk.
   looked / refrigerator?
6 I've hurt my knee.
   been / doctor?
7 I've forgotten Bob's telephone number.
   looked / telephone directory?
8 I've had a headache all day.
   taken / aspirin?

READING COMPREHENSION

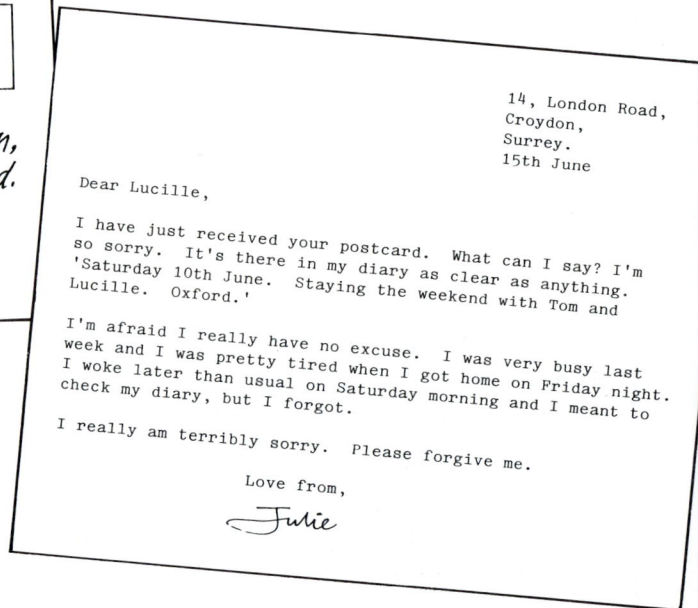

POST CARD

Tom and I were
expecting you
for the weekend.
Sorry you couldn't
come. Hope you
aren't ill.

+Lucille

Mrs. Julie Brown,
14 London Road.
Croydon,
SURREY.

14, London Road,
Croydon,
Surrey.
15th June

Dear Lucille,

I have just received your postcard. What can I say? I'm
so sorry. It's there in my diary as clear as anything.
'Saturday 10th June. Staying the weekend with Tom and
Lucille. Oxford.'

I'm afraid I really have no excuse. I was very busy last
week and I was pretty tired when I got home on Friday night.
I woke later than usual on Saturday morning and I meant to
check my diary, but I forgot.

I really am terribly sorry. Please forgive me.

Love from,

Julie

D   Questions

1 Who wrote the letter?
2 Why must the writer apologise?
3 Ask where Tom and Lucille live.
4 Answer the question.
5 How did Julie feel on Friday night?
6 Ask if she checked her diary on
   Saturday morning.
7 Answer the question.

LISTENING ACTIVITIES

E   Listen to the tape.

	True	False	Don't know
1 Julie is calling from her house.			
2 Bob's number is Croydon 652.			
3 Julie is in London.			
4 Julie's train was late.			
5 Julie is late.			
6 Julie can't go to Croydon.			
7 Julie is apologising.			
8 Bob is angry.			

GRAMMAR SUMMARY

F   Note these useful ways of apologising:

I'm sorry . . .
I'm very sorry . . .
I really am terribly sorry . . .

Note, too, how we can forgive somebody:
Never mind . . .
Don't worry about it . . .

We use the **present perfect** tense when we are talking about
something that has just happened. Here are the forms.

Statements

I You	have	
He/she	has	(just) *received* a postcard from Lucille.
We You They	have	

Negatives

I You	haven't	
He/she	hasn't	*received* a postcard from Bob.
We You They	haven't	

Questions

Have	you	
Has	he/she	(just) *received* a postcard from Lucille?
Have	we you they	

Special note: We never use the **present perfect** when we are
interested in *when* something happened.

Compare: *I've received a card from Lucille.*
            I received a card from Lucille yesterday.

G   Practise beginning letters.

Example: You have just received a postcard. Begin a letter
to Lucille Jones. ('I'm so sorry.')

Dear Lucille,
I have just received your postcard. I'm so sorry.

Continue in the same way (you know each of these people and so
you can use their first names.)

1 You have just seen a new film, *Jungle Moon*. Begin a letter
to Sam Sprott, the producer. ('I think the film is
marvellous.')

2 You have just read an article about prisons in *The Times*.
Begin a letter to Maggie Priest, the writer. ('I agree with
you completely.')

3 You have just heard a new record, *Earth Song*. Begin a
letter to Chris Jackson, the drummer. ('I think the record is
tremendous.')

4 You have just listened to a talk on the radio about
telepathy. Begin a letter to the speaker, Professor
Anderson. ('I am sure you are right.')

5 You have just watched a programme about Bali on
television. Begin a letter to Dick Jenkins, the
photographer. ('I think the photography was superb.')

6 You have just read a book sent to you by your friend
Mark. Begin the letter to him. ('I found the book very
interesting.')

**H   Anthea arranged to meet Tom yesterday afternoon but
she felt ill and couldn't go. Here is the letter of apology she
wrote the next day. Fill in the missing words.**

Dear Tom,

I_____terribly_____I couldn't meet you as I promised yesterday.

I didn't_____well yesterday and I couldn't go out. I_____you

several times, but nobody answered. I_____you didn't wait for me.

Please_____ _____ .

_____ _____,

Anthea

HOMEWORK EXERCISES

A   Do you remember the lady who left her handbag in the cinema?

She said: I've left my handbag inside.

Look at the pictures and practise making remarks like this. (Put the verbs into the present perfect tense.)

1

TOM	Can I have a cloth?
MARY	Why ?
TOM	spill/tea

2

MAN A	Come on. What are you doing?
MAN B	lose/ball

3

POLICEMAN	May I ask what you are doing, Sir?
PETER	forget/key

B   You accepted an invitation to have supper with a friend on Tuesday evening. You forgot about it and have just received a postcard from your friend:

'Sorry you could not come to supper, as we arranged. Laura.'

Write a short letter in reply. Include your own address and the date.

C   Dictation

Dear Mr Scott,

   Thank you for your letter of 15th January. You say that you telephoned our office five times in two days and did not receive a reply.

   I am sorry about this, but we have had problems with our telephone.

                    Yours sincerely,
                    D. Renton

STUDY THE WORDS

Study these words (look at the Dialogue):

Jobs:
bank clerk
optician
dentist
doorman
photographer
producer

Other words in this unit (can you find them?):

weekend	reception	purse
superb	library	tooth
pretty	telephone	headache
tired	directory	yours sincerely
angry	banker's card	glasses
refrigerator	receipt	
cloth	handbag	

1 Frank does the same things from Monday to Friday. He gets up at 7 o'clock, has a shower, eats an apple and runs to the station. He arrives at work about ten minutes late. Yesterday was Tuesday. Write what Frank did.

1 He _____ at 7 o'clock.
2 Then he _____ a shower.
3 He _____ an apple.
4 And then he _____ to the station.
5 He _____ about ten minutes late.

2 Your friend has a new watch. You like it very much. You ask some questions about it. Read your friend's answers and then write your questions.

YOU   _____
YOUR FRIEND   I didn't buy it. It was a present.

YOU   _____
YOUR FRIEND   My parents.

YOU   _____
YOUR FRIEND   Yes, I'm afraid it was very expensive.

YOU   _____
YOUR FRIEND   Because I had a birthday last week.

YOU   _____
YOUR FRIEND   Oh, yes, I enjoyed it very much.

3 Now look at these verbs and read the questions. Put a circle round the letter for the missing verb. Here is an example.

Example:

A is   **B** have   **C** do   (**D**)did   **E** are

What time _____ you   A B C D E
get up this morning?

A is   **B** have   **C** do   **D** did   **E** are

1 What ___ your name?   A B C D E
2 Where ___ you come from?   A B C D E
3 Where ___ you go yesterday?   A B C D E
4 What ___ you lost?   A B C D E
5 ___ you like football?   A B C D E
6 What ___ you going to do now?   A B C D E
7 ___ you enjoy your holiday?   A B C D E
8 ___ you got any stamps?   A B C D E
9 ___ you going to have a shower?   A B C D E
10 ___ this your sweater?   A B C D E

4 Write what you could say in these situations:

1 You are looking for the football ground. You say: 'Excuse me, _____ ?'
2 You want to know what time the match starts. You say: '_____ ?'
3 You want to invite your friend to the match on Saturday. You say: '_____ ?'
4 Your friend doesn't like football. She says, 'I think football is awful.' You don't agree. You say: '_____ ?'
5 You forget to meet your friend. You telephone and apologise. You say: '_____ '

You have to put the soap powder in here

Klaus is using the launderette for the first time.

KLAUS   Excuse me, do you know how this works?
HOUSEWIFE   Yes. Put the washing inside . . . shut the door
               . . . the money goes in here, then when the
               machine starts you have to put the soap
               powder in through here.
KLAUS   Is that all?
HOUSEWIFE   Yes, you don't have to do anything else until
               the machine stops.
KLAUS   Thank you.

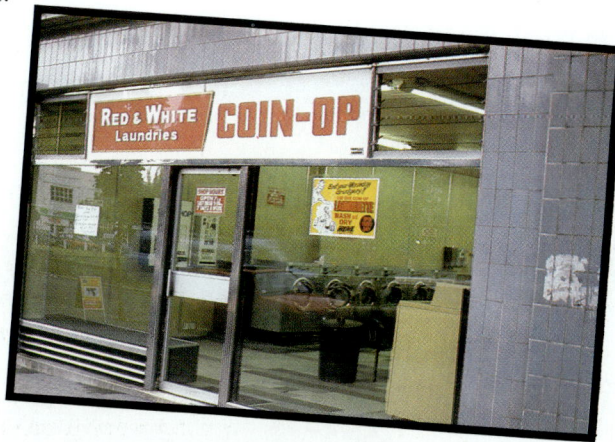

A   Questions

1 Where is Klaus?
2 Who else is there?
3 Where is Klaus going to put his washing?
4 Does he have to put the soap powder in before the
  machine stops?
5 Do you have to pay to use the launderette?
6 What is Klaus going to do when the machine stops?

B   Study this sentence:

You have to buy a ticket.

Now practise using **have to.**

1 Before you go into the cinema/a ticket
2 Before you drink a can of Coca-Cola/the can
3 Before you can become a doctor/an examination
4 Before you get a driving licence/a test
5 In order to travel to some countries/a visa

C Notice these two ways of expressing the same idea:

It isn't necessary to do anything else.
You don't have to do anything else.

It isn't necessary for her to worry about money.
She doesn't have to worry about money.

Now express the following ideas, using **dont have to** *or* **doesn't have to** *instead of* **isn't necessary.**

1 It isn't necessary for her to work. She gets a pension.
2 It isn't necessary for us to buy a new car just now. This one is all right.
3 It isn't necessary for him to find a new job immediately. He has a lot of money.
4 It isn't necessary for me to work very hard on a Sunday. We don't get many customers.
5 It isn't necessary for them to live in that small flat. They could easily buy a house.

D Discussion

Think of some things you have to do; things you don't like perhaps.

Think of some things you *don't* have to do, but which other people have to do.

ideas: a bus driver
a hospital nurse
a travelling salesman
a politician
a princess

BEECHWOOD MANOR Health Farm

You are looking at this advertisement, so you are probably interested in losing a little weight but you don't want to suffer too much doing it.

We can help you lose those extra kilos and at the same time we can offer you a healthy, active holiday in a beautiful old house standing in the middle of a splendid park.

You can swim in our fine indoor pool, play tennis on our magnificent hard courts or work out in our first class gymnasium and believe it or not – you don't have to give up eating either. The food is delicious.

Interested?
Then give us a ring at 699 1234 or fill in the enclosed coupon and post if off today.

Name _____

Address _____

_____

I want to lose weight and enjoy doing it. Please send me details by return of post.

E   Questions

1 Why do people answer this advertisement?
2 What game can the people play?
3 What other kinds of exercise can they take?
4 Why is it surprising that they don't have to give up eating?
5 How can people get more information about these holidays?

F   Here are the instructions Bob gives Julie:

First you have to buy a film.

Now look and listen.

Press the release.

Open the film compartment.

Close the film compartment.

Put a film cartridge in the compartment.

Look through the viewfinder.

Push the lever until you see number 1.

Press the button.

```
1
```

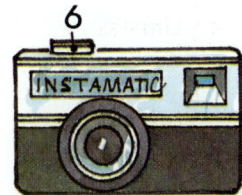

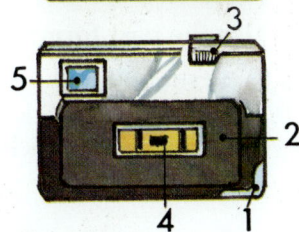

① release
② film compartment
③ lever
④ counter window
⑤ viewfinder
⑥ button

GRAMMAR SUMMARY

Statements

I You	have to	
He/she	has to	get the tickets.
We You They	have to	

Negatives

I You	don't		
He/she	doesn't	have to	get the tickets.
We You They	don't		

Questions

Do	I you				I you	do.
Does	he/she	have to	get the tickets?	Yes	he/she	does.
Do	we you they				you we they	do.

Note also the past forms:

I *had to* get the tickets.
I *didn't have to* get the tickets.
Did you *have to* get the tickets.

HOMEWORK EXERCISES

A

1 You arrive in a foreign country. What do you have to show to the immigration officer?
2 What do you have to have before you fly to Hong Kong?
3 What do you have to do to get a driving licence?
4 How long does a doctor have to study in your country?

B   Look at this example:

It wasn't necessary for her to work.
She didn't have to work.

Continue in the same way:

1 It wasn't necessary for him to find a new job at once.
2 It wasn't necessary for us to take a taxi.
3 It wasn't necessary for you to bring any money.
4 It wasn't necessary for you to pay the bill.

C   Dictation

Have you ever thought what it is like to be one of those beautiful girls that you see on the front of fashion magazines?

   They meet interesting people, they travel to exciting places, and sometimes they make a lot of money. But they have to work hard. They often have to get up very early in the morning, and of course they have to be very careful about what they eat.

STUDY THE WORDS

Remember these words (look at the Dialogue):

The launderette:
launderette
washing
soap powder
washing machine

Jobs:
boss
nurse
salesman
princess
politician
soldier

Remember these words (look at the Reading comprehension):

A healthy holiday:
healthy   magnificent
active   delicious
middle   gymnasium
pool

Other words in this unit (can you find them?):

driving licence   immediately
test   light reading
visa   coupon
pension   immigration officer

Would you have a look at this watch, please?

DIALOGUE

ASSISTANT Good morning.

TIM Good morning. Would you have a look at this watch, please? It doesn't keep good time.

ASSISTANT Yes, of course.

The assistant takes the watch to be examined. Then he returns.

ASSISTANT There's nothing seriously wrong. It only needs cleaning.

TIM I see. Can you give me an estimate?

ASSISTANT It'll cost about £5.

TIM And how long will it take?

ASSISTANT About a fortnight.

TIM Thank you . . .

A Questions

1 Why is Tim worried about his watch?
2 What did the assistant do?
3 Is there anything seriously wrong with the watch?
4 What does it need?
5 Tim asks for an estimate. What does this mean?
6 How long will it take to clean the watch?

B Note what Tim says:

'Good morning. Would you have a look at this watch, please? It doesn't keep good time.'

'Good morning. Would you have a look at this cassette recorder, please? It isn't recording.'

What would you say when you take these things to be repaired?

1 electric kettle/not getting hot
2 hair dryer/getting terribly hot
3 toaster/burning the toast
4 iron/overheating
5 table lamp/not working
6 record player/going round at the wrong speed

C Study this part of the conversation.

TIM	Can you give me an estimate?
ASSISTANT	It'll cost about £5.
TIM	How long will it take?
ASSISTANT	About a fortnight.
TIM	All right. Thank you.

Practise conversations like this:

1 Ask about the alarm clock. (£2.50/3 weeks)

2 Ask about the cassette recorder. (£2/a week)

3 Ask about the kettle. (£5/a week)

4 Ask about the hair dryer. (£1/a week)

5 Ask about the toaster. (£4/3 weeks)

6 Ask about the iron. (£4/a month)

7 Ask about the table lamp. (£2/3 days)

8 Ask about the radio. (£3/a week)

D Sometimes you may decide that the price of the repair is too high. Then you can say:

'Mm, that's rather a lot. I'd like to think about it.'

Now, decide to accept or reject the following estimates.

Example:

YOU	Can you give me an estimate to repair this hair dryer?
ASSISTANT	It'll cost about £4.
YOU	All right, thank you. *or*
	Mm, that's rather a lot. I'd like to think about it.

1 YOU   Can you give me an estimate to repair this watch?
  ASSISTANT   It'll cost about £6.
  YOU   _____

2 YOU   Can you give me an estimate to repair this kettle?
  ASSISTANT   It'll cost about £1.
  YOU   _____

3 YOU   Can you give me an estimate to repair this camera?
  ASSISTANT   It'll cost about £15.
  YOU   _____

4 YOU   Can you give me an estimate to repair this typewriter?
  ASSISTANT   It'll cost about £5.
  YOU   _____

5 YOU   Can you give me an estimate to repair this ring?
  ASSISTANT   It'll cost about £10.
  YOU   _____

6 YOU   Can you give me an estimate to repair this radio?
    ASSISTANT   It'll cost about £2.
    YOU   _____

7 YOU   Can you give me an estimate to repair this
                    pearl necklace?
    ASSISTANT   It'll cost about £2.
    YOU   _____

8 YOU   Can you give me an estimate to repair this iron?
    ASSISTANT   It'll cost about £8.
    YOU   _____

READING COMPREHENSION

My name is Mr Porter. When I was about sixteen, we had a big, old-fashioned radio. One day the radio stopped working. I removed the back and looked inside. It didn't look very complicated but I could not repair it. So I had to carry it to the shop. It was very heavy.

Now I have a colour television. Last week it stopped working. I rang the shop and a young man came to repair it. The inside of the television looked terribly complicated. But the young man removed a piece of brown plastic covered with very small green and red wires. He replaced this part. Then he put the television together again, turned it on and it worked beautifully.

E Questions

1 What was Mr Porter's radio like?
2 How did he know what the inside was like?
3 What did he do with the radio?
4 What did the young man come to do?
5 Which was more complicated, the radio or the television?

GRAMMAR SUMMARY

F This unit will teach you what to say when you take something to be repaired.

Note: Would you have a look at this _____, please?
        Can you give me an estimate to repair this _____?
        How long will it take?

Remember also how to accept or reject an estimate.

All right, thank you. *or*
Mm, that's rather a lot. I'd like to think about it.

Note also the useful verbs:

to lend and *to borrow*   I *lent* my bicycle *to* George.
                         He *borrowed* it *from* me.

LISTENING ACTIVITIES

G   Listen to the tape.

Example:

WOMAN   How much will it cost to repair this typewriter?
ASSISTANT   About _____ .
WOMAN   That's not bad. But how long will it take?
ASSISTANT   Only about _____ .

Dialogue a

CUSTOMER   Can you give me an estimate to repair this bicycle?
ASSISTANT   I think it'll cost about _____ or _____ .
CUSTOMER   And how long will it take?
ASSISTANT   _____ , more or less.

Dialogue b

CUSTOMER   Would you have a look at this television set, please?
ASSISTANT   Yes, of course. _____ _____ have you had it?
CUSTOMER   About _____ _____ . Can you tell me how much it'll cost to repair it?
ASSISTANT   Well, the set is very old. It'll cost about _____ . It's _____ to buy a new one.

Dialogue c

CUSTOMER   How much do you think it'll cost to repair this typewriter?
ASSISTANT   Let me see. It's a _____ model. About _____ , I'm afraid.
CUSTOMER   That's rather a lot. And how long will it take?
ASSISTANT   About _____ .
CUSTOMER   Thank you. I'd like to think about it.

Dialogue d

You have done this before. Choose the best answer when you listen to the conversation.

Choose: *True, False,* or *Don't know.*

	True	False	Don't know
1 Tony has left his typewriter in the shop.			
2 Tony thinks £20 is expensive.			
3 Tony has one typewriter.			
4 Bob wants to borrow a typewriter.			
5 Tony lends Bob a typewriter.			

H   Tim wanted the assistant to look at his watch, so he said:

'Would you have a look at this watch, please?'

Sometimes we begin requests with: 'Could you . . .?'

Example: 'Could you pass me the sugar, please?'

Practise:

1 You want the butter.
2 You want your friend to lend you a pen.
3 You want your friend to turn down the radio.
4 You want your friend to get some milk.
5 You want your friend to turn on the television.
6 You want someone to tell you the time.
7 You want to have another piece of cake.
8 You want to borrow your friend's calculator.
9 You want someone to move his car.
10 You want your friend to give you a lift to the station.

I   Note what David says:

' . . . I lent it to my young brother.'

David *lent* the cassette recorder to his brother. So his brother *borrowed* it from him.

*Practise using **lent** and **borrowed**:*

1 George borrowed your calculator.   So you . . .
2 You borrowed George's pen.   So he . . .
3 Pam borrowed Kathy's hair dryer.   So Kathy . . .
4 But Pam lent her electric kettle to Kathy.   So Kathy . . .
5 George lent his alarm clock to Tim.   So Tim . . .
6 Pam lent her iron to Tim.   So Tim . . .
7 But Pam borrowed Tim's typewriter.   So Tim . . .
8 Tim also lent his typewriter to George.   So George . . .

HOMEWORK EXERCISES

A

1 You have a hair dryer. It's not working. You bought it two years ago. You take it back to the shop where you bought it. What do you say?
2 The assistant tells you they can repair it. He says you have to come back in a week. But he doesn't say anything about the price. What do you say?
3 The assistant tells you how much the repair will cost. You think the price is too high. What do you say?
4 What do you say, if the assistant gives you an estimate and you decide to accept it?

B   You are sitting at the table. It's tea-time. Ask politely . . .

1 Your cup is empty. You want some more tea.
2 The jam is on the other side of the table. You want some.
3 You want another piece of chocolate cake.
4 You want the butter.
5 You want a biscuit.

C   Lend and borrow
Put the correct word in the gaps.

Tom wanted to buy a record, but he didn't have enough money. But George _____ him £5 and Tom bought the record. Then George said: 'I _____ you the money, so I want you to _____ me the record for a few days.' So George _____ the record and he played it many times. When Tom got it back, it was badly scratched. Tom looked at it sadly. 'I'm never going to _____ anyone my records again,' he said.

D   Dictation

I have a watch. It is a Swiss watch. It is not new and my friends are sometimes a little rude about it. They tell me to buy a new one. But I do not want a new one. I am very happy with my old watch.

   Last week it stopped. So I took it to the shop. I did not ask for an estimate. Today I went to get it. Do you know how much I had to pay? £5. £5 just for cleaning a watch.

STUDY THE WORDS

Remember these words (look at the Dialogue):

Useful things in the home:

alarm clock	table lamp
electric kettle	plastic
hair dryer	wires
toaster	calculator
iron	typewriter

People can be:
wrong
old-fashioned
similar
rude

Other words in this unit (can you find them?):

estimate	seriously
fortnight	complicated
speed	scratched
ring	heavy
pearl necklace	replace
simply	

Let's have a party

DIALOGUE	

GABY	Let's have a party.
EDWARD	What a good idea. When shall we have it?
GABY	What about Saturday evening?
EDWARD	Fine, and where shall we have it?
GABY	In your flat.
EDWARD	Oh, you know what my landlady's like. She won't let us have a party there.
GABY	Let's ask Doris. Perhaps we can have it in her flat.

A Questions

1 What does Gaby want to do?
2 Does Edward think it's a good idea?
3 When are they going to have the party?
4 Where does Gaby want to have the party?
5 What are they going to ask Doris?

B Doris says:

'All right. You can have the party in my flat, but my record player isn't very good. Edward, will you bring your record player?'
  Edward says: 'Yes, I'll bring some records too.'
  Gaby says: 'Shall I bring some glasses?'

Think of some more things that Gaby, Edward and Doris might say, beginning: **Will you . . . ?, I'll . . . ,** *or* **Shall I . . . ?**

Ideas: lemonade   Beatles LP
    ice cream   cassette recorder
    orange juice   some cassettes
    fruit   guitar

C Gaby says: *'Shall I get some invitations?'*

Now you offer to help.

Example: You have just finished a game of tennis. You both feel thirsty.
      YOU SAY: _____ orange juice?
          Shall I get some orange juice?

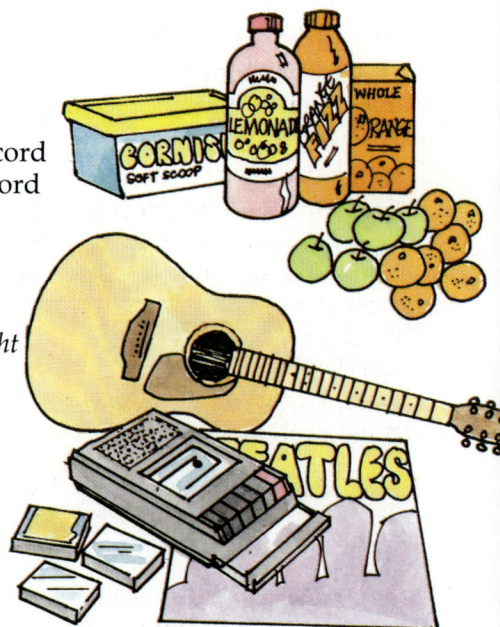

Continue in the same way:

1 You spent the morning shopping with a friend. You have just got home and you're hungry.
YOU SAY: _____ sandwiches?

2 You work in the same office as Doris. There is bad news. Her boy friend has been hurt in an accident. Someone must tell her.
YOU SAY: _____ tell _____ ?

3 You and a friend want to go to the theatre. Someone must get the tickets.
YOU SAY: _____ tickets?

4 Your friend is trying to open a bottle of wine and having problems.
YOU SAY: _____ open _____ ?

5 Rita is finding it difficult to start her car. You know a lot about cars.
YOU SAY: _____ start _____ ?

6 Pat and Christine are arguing about who is going to post the letters. You are going past the post office.
YOU SAY: _____ post _____ ?

7 The person you share a flat with can't find his/her key. You aren't going out.
YOU SAY: _____ lend _____ ?

8 You have just had a very nice meal with a friend. The waiter comes up with the bill. You are feeling generous.
YOU SAY: _____ pay _____ ?

✳ D   Here are some more situations. Offer to help. Use: 'I'll . . .'

Example: The telephone's ringing. (answer)   I'll answer it.

1 Oh, dear, I've forgotten to bring any money. (lend)
2 My goodness, I'm thirsty. (get)
3 There isn't any more milk. (buy)
4 Goodness, it's hot in here. (open)
5 Oh, dear, I haven't got a stamp. (give)
6 There's somebody at the door. (answer)
7 It's very dark in here. (switch on)
8 I'd like to hear the news. (turn on)

E   Edward says: *'She won't let us have a party there'*!
We say: *'won't'*, but we write *'will not'*.

Look at this example:
Tom will not work on Saturday.   Tom won't work on Saturday.

Continue in the same way:

1 Susan will not be early tomorrow.
2 I'm afraid Peter will not lend you his records.
3 Mary will not go to the post office with that parcel.
4 Frank will not get the tickets.
5 Tom will not take Sally to the station.
6 Kathy will not type those letters today.

LISTENING ACTIVITIES

F   Listen to the tape and follow the instructions.

	making a suggestion	asking for advice	making a request	making an offer
Activity 1				
a The woman is:				
b The man is:				
c The woman is:				
d The man is:				
Activity 2				
a The man is:				
b The woman is:				
c The man is:				
d The woman is:				
Activity 3				
a The woman is:				
b The man is:				
c The woman is:				
d The man is:				
Activity 4				
a The woman is:				
b The man is:				
c The woman is:				
d The man is:				

READING COMPREHENSION

Ted wanted a car very much, but he didn't have much money. He saw a ten-year-old Cortina for a hundred and fifty pounds and he asked me to go with him to buy it.

'Cash only,' said the dealer.

'That's all right,' said Ted, 'I'll pay cash.'

'That's fine then,' replied the dealer.

Half an hour later Ted drove the old Cortina out of the showroom and down towards the traffic lights.

I'm not sure what happened next. Ted says the brakes didn't work. Perhaps he wasn't careful enough, but he drove straight into the back of a 185 bus. The driver wasn't very pleased and the front of the Cortina was in a terrible state.

We took the car back. The dealer looked at it and shook his head. He couldn't believe it.

'The brakes didn't work,' said Ted.

'I checked them myself this morning,' said the dealer.

'Can you do anything?' asked Ted.

'I'll buy it back, if you like.'

'How much will you give me?'

'The repairs will cost a hundred pounds. I'll give you fifty pounds.'

The car is still standing outside Ted's house.

G   Questions

 1 How much was the Cortina?
 2 Was it new?
 3 How did Ted pay for it?
 4 Why do you think Ted drove into the back of the bus?
 5 What reason did Ted give for driving into the bus?
 6 What did the dealer do to the brakes?
 7 How did the bus driver feel about the accident?
 8 What did the dealer offer to do?
 9 How much was he willing to pay?
10 Did Ted sell the Cortina?

GRAMMAR SUMMARY

H   We often use the **simple future** when we offer to carry out some useful action.

Example:
Shall I get some invitations?
I'll pay cash.
I'll buy it back, if you like.

The **negative form** is useful too:
Tom won't work on Saturday.
I'm afraid Mr Scott won't see you now.

And we often use the **question form** when we ask people to do things for us.

Will you shut the door, please?
Will you get me some stamps?

Here are the forms:

Statements

I You He/she We You They	'll (will)	make some tea.

Negatives

I You He/she We You They	won't (will not)	make any tea.

Questions

Shall	I	
Will	you he/she	make some tea?
Shall	we	
Will	you they	

I   Ted asked the dealer this question:

'How much will you give me?'

You are in the office of a travel agent asking about your flight from London to Australia via Hong Kong. Practise asking questions with 'will'.

1 You want to know which airport you will fly from.
   Which _____ ?
2 You want to know how much it will cost.
   How much _____ ?
3 You want to know how long it will take to get to Hong Kong.
   How long _____ ?

4 You want to know how much sleep you will get during the flight.
How much _____ ?

5 You want to know which countries you will pass over.
Which countries _____ ?

6 You want to know how much time you will have to look round Hong Kong.
How much _____ ?

7 You want to know which hotel you will stay at in Hong Kong.
Which hotel _____ ?

8 You want to know when you will arrive in Australia.
When _____ ?

J We often use the *simple future* when asking people to do things.

Example: You feel cold.
        YOU SAY: Will you please close the window?
Continue in the same way:

1 It's rather dark in the sitting room.
YOU SAY: _____

2 Your friend has his radio on too loud.
YOU SAY: _____

3 There is no salt on the table. Your friend is just going into the kitchen.
YOU SAY: _____

4 It's cold in the sitting room.
YOU SAY: _____

5 You need some stamps. Your friend is going near the post office.
YOU SAY: _____

6 Your friend has a book you would like to borrow.
YOU SAY: _____

7 Your friend is going shopping. You would like to see a newspaper.
YOU SAY: _____

8 You want your friend to help you move the piano.
YOU SAY: _____

HOMEWORK EXERCISES

A Offer to do things, using *Shall I . . . ?*

1 Offer to make some sandwiches.
2 Offer to telephone for a taxi.
3 Offer to get the tickets.
4 Offer to post a letter for a friend.
5 Offer to take a photograph of your friends standing in front of their new car.

B Offer to help using *I'll* . . .

1 It's cold in the sitting room.
2 You think your friend would like a cup of coffee.
3 You are sure your friend would like to watch the news on the television.
4 You think a friend would like to borrow a book of yours.
5 Your friend likes music. You have a new record.

C You are in the office of a travel agent. You are going from London to Paris for a weekend holiday. Ask questions with *'will'*.

1 You want to know the price.
   How much _____?
2 You want to know where you will stay.
   Where _____?
3 You want to know what time you will arrive in Paris.
   What time _____?
4 You want to know how many people there will be in the group.
   How many _____?
5 You want to know when you will arrive back in London.
   When _____?

D Dictation

> Dear Gaby,
>   Thank you for your invitation to the party next weekend. I would like to come very much. Unfortunately I have not got many records but I will bring two LPs by the Beatles. I think you will like them.
>   I have to work on Saturday so I am afraid I will be a little late.
>   Love from,
>   George.

STUDY THE WORDS

Remember these words (look at the Dialogue):

The party:

record player	invitation
lemonade	hungry
orange juice	thirsty
LP	piano

Remember these words (look at the Reading comprehension):

Buying a car:

generous	terrible
cash	dealer
showroom	careful
brakes	accident

Hello, I'd like to speak to Frieda, please

MRS PEACH	698 3456 Hello, Mrs Peach here . . .
STAN	Hello, it's Stan. I'd like to speak to Frieda please.
MRS PEACH	Hold on . . . I'll see if she's in . . . No, I'm afraid she's out.
STAN	Could you ask her to ring me back?
MRS PEACH	Yes, of course, what's your number?
STAN	231 4796.
MRS PEACH	All right. Bye . . .

A   Questions

1 Who does Stan want to speak to?
2 Who answers the phone?
3 Does Mrs Peach fetch Frieda?
4 Why not?
5 What does Stan want Frieda to do?
6 What does Mrs Peach ask Stan for?

B   Stan asks to speak to Frieda.

Mrs Peach says: 'I'm afraid she's out.'
Stan's friend Peter rings and asks to speak to Helena.
Mrs Brown says: 'Hold on a moment. I'll get her.'

Practise conversations like this:

1 GEORGE   Hello, could I speak to Peter, please? (out)
  YOU   _____
2 TOM   Hello, could I speak to Sally? (in)
  YOU   _____
3 FRIEDA   Hello, I'd like to speak to Ted. Is he there? (in)
  YOU   _____
4 TED   Ted here. Can I speak to Tom? (out)
  YOU   _____
5 DORIS   Hello, could I speak to Ted? (in)
  YOU   _____
6 PETER   Hello, I'd like to speak to Tom. Is he there? (in)
  YOU   _____
7 KLAUS   Hello, could I speak to Frieda? (out)
  YOU   _____
8 DAVID   Hello, can I speak to George, please? (out)
  YOU   _____

C   Frieda rings Stan.

STAN   231 4796.

FRIEDA   Can I speak to Stan, please?

STAN   Stan speaking.

FRIEDA   Hello, it's Frieda. You rang me earlier.

STAN   Yes, I did. Would you like to come to the cinema this evening?

FRIEDA   I'm afraid I can't this evening. I'm busy.

STAN   What about tomorrow evening then?

FRIEDA   That would be lovely. What time?

Invite a friend to:

1 the theatre
2 a football match
3 a party
4 a pop concert

You want your friend to go:

5 swimming with you
6 shopping
7 dancing
8 sailing

D   When we ring somebody who works for a big firm, the switchboard operator usually puts us through to the person we want to speak to.

SWITCHBOARD
OPERATOR   Parker Products Limited.

STAN   Could I please speak to Miss Julie Hearn, extension 231, please?

SWITCHBOARD
OPERATOR   Hold on please . . . You're through . . .

JULIE   Julie Hearn speaking.

STAN   Hello, I saw your advertisement in *Melody Maker* . . .

Practise conversations like this (You don't always know the extension number):

1 You want to speak to John Gifford of Parker Products Limited. (extension 132)
2 You want to speak to George Roberts, of Roberts and Company.
3 You want to speak to Joy Smith of E. R. Johnson Limited. (extension 34)
4 You want to speak to Bernard Hopkins of Palmer and Hopkins. (extension 6)
5 You want to speak to Roger Clarke of W. Williams Limited.
6 You want to speak to Mary Purser of the *Daily Record.*

READING COMPREHENSION

In my office I have a grey telephone and at home I have a black one. They both work very well and they are very useful.

But last week I passed a shop and I noticed that the window was full of telephones. There were green telephones, blue telephones, red telephones, big telephones, small telephones and one elegant gold telephone. 'Why?' I thought. 'What are they all for? Are there people who have a different kind of telephone in every room?'

Then this morning in the paper I read about a new sort of telephone. It has a screen so that you can not only speak to the other person, but see him as well. That really is a very clever idea. But I'm not going to buy one. I am quite happy with my old black telephone.

E   Questions

1 Does the writer sometimes use the telephone?
2 What did the writer see last week that surprised him?
3 How did the writer find out about the new sort of telephone?
4 What is special about this new sort of telephone?
5 Would you like to have one like this?
6 Can you think of any possible disadvantages?

GRAMMAR SUMMARY

F   Here is a list of useful phrases:

When you phone somebody:
Hello, I'd like to speak to . . .
Hello, can I speak to . . . please?
Could you ask her to ring me back, please?

When you answer the phone:
Hold on please, I'll get him/her.
Hold on please, I'll see if she's in.
I'm afraid she's out.

When you're inviting somebody to go out with you:
Would you like to come (to) . . . ?

When you have been asked to go out with somebody:
That would be lovely.
I'm afraid I can't this evening. I'm busy.

When you ring a theatre or booking office:
Have you got any tickets for . . . ?
I'd like to reserve two seats at . . . , please.

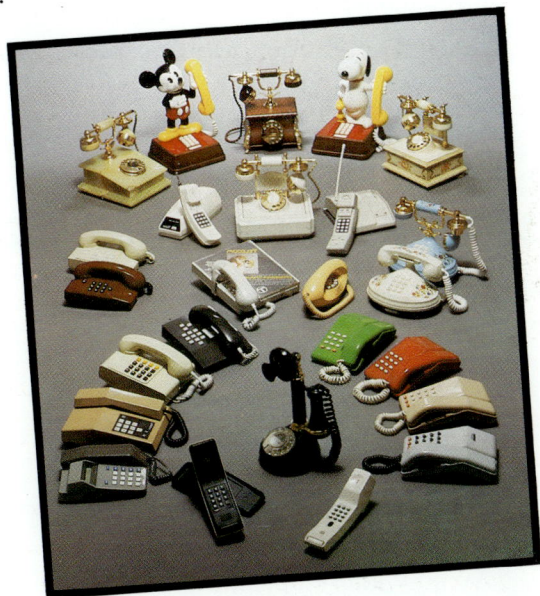

G   Listen and write

CLERK   Cambridge Theatre. Box Office.

HENRY   Have you got any tickets for *Romeo and Juliet* _____ _____ _____ evening?

CLERK   Which performance? 5 pm or 8.30 pm?

HENRY   _____ _____, please.

CLERK   Sorry, that performance is _____ _____ .

HENRY   Well, have you got _____ _____ for the 5 pm performance?

CLERK   Yes, we have tickets at _____, _____ and £6.

HENRY   _____ _____ _____ reserve two seats at £4.50, please.

CLERK   Right. That's two tickets at £4.50. Saturday, 5 pm performance. _____ _____ _____, please?

HENRY   Bishop. Henry Bishop.

CLERK   Thank you. _____ collect the tickets before 3 pm on Saturday, _____ _____ ?

HENRY   Yes, of course. Thank you. Goodbye.

✳ H   Gaby wants to make a telephone call to a friend from a public telephone box.

GABY   Excuse me, I want to make a phone call. Can you help me?

FRANK   Of course. Have you got your money ready?

GABY   What do I need?

FRANK   A 10p piece.

GABY   Yes, I've got one.

FRANK   Lift the receiver, dial the number you want and wait for the pips . . .

GABY   The pips?

FRANK   Yes, when the other person answers, you'll hear pip . . . pip . . . pip . . . then you put your money in and speak. OK?

GABY   Lovely . . . thanks.

Now answer these questions:

1 What does Gaby want to do?
2 Where does she want to make the call from?
3 How much money is she going to put in?
4 What must she do with the receiver?
5 What number must she dial?
6 Then what must she wait for?
7 What must she do when she hears the pips?
8 What will she be able to do then?

HOMEWORK EXERCISES

A

1 John and Tom share a flat. The telephone rings. Somebody wants to speak to Tom. Tom isn't in. What does John say?

2 The next day the telephone rings again. Somebody says: 'Can I speak to Tom, please?' Tom is in his room. What does John say?

3 You telephone a friend. You want to invite your friend to come to the cinema with you tomorrow evening. What do you say?

4 Your friend wants to come with you to the cinema. What does he/she say?

5 How would you refuse an invitation to go to the cinema, politely?

6 You want to speak to Peter Perkins, of Rose and Co. He gave you his card. You telephone him. What do you say when his secretary answers the phone?

B   You want two tickets for *Holiday on Ice* **on Saturday evening. You ring the theatre. Complete this conversation:**

YOU   Have you_____?
CLERK   Yes, we have tickets at £3, £4, and £6.
YOU   _____ reserve _____
CLERK   Right, That's _____ tickets at _____ for _____. What's the name, please?
YOU   _____

C   Dictation

People often ask me for my telephone number. But I have not got a telephone, so I tell them to ring me at work.

Why do I not have a telephone? I think the telephone is expensive and I prefer to write a letter. There are not many people I want to speak to in the evening and I do not want to speak to anybody at breakfast time.

When I want to use the telephone in the evening, I can always use the box at the end of the road.

STUDY THE WORDS

Remember these words (can you find them?):

elegant	the pips	disadvantage	extension
special	kind of	different	receiver
available	screen	switchboard	polite
really	advantage	operator	

Frank's getting married

DIALOGUE

TERRY   Frank's getting married.
JAMES   Is he really?
TERRY   Yes he is.
JAMES   I don't believe it.
TERRY   It's true.
JAMES   Who's he marrying?
TERRY   A girl he met on holiday in Spain I think.
JAMES   Good heavens . . . where are they going to live?

A Questions

1 Why is James surprised?
2 Ask who Frank is marrying.
3 Ask where he met her.
4 Answer the question.
5 Ask where they are going to live.

B Study this pattern:

Frank/get/married.
Frank's getting married.

Make more sentences like this:

1 My sister/give/a party at the weekend
2 Edward/come/to the party
3 He/lend/us his record player
4 He/bring/some records too
5 John/organise/some games

C Here is a list of people:

1 The bank manager and his wife.
2 John, who is sixteen, and his friend, Peter.
3 Harry, the bus conductor.
4 Harry's wife, Ethel.
5 Professor Thomas Finkenstein.
6 George, who is 21, single, and rather good-looking.
7 Alice and Brenda, who are both 17, and work in
  a big store.
8 Ginger Parker, the drummer with a pop group.

This is what they are doing on Saturday. You have to decide who is doing what.

a They are going to a football match.
b They are going to the theatre.
c He is taking Paulette Johnson to the pictures.
d He is having dinner with a well-known art historian and his wife.
e He's working late this evening.
f She's staying in this evening.
g He's playing at the Rainbow Theatre tonight.
h They are going to a disco.

Answers:

1 _____   3 _____   5 _____   7 _____
2 _____   4 _____   6 _____   8 _____

D   Some people think that beauty contests are very silly and degrading to women. But when the Miss World contest is shown on television, millions of people watch, and of course the girl who wins has a very busy year.

You are Miss World's personal manager and you must discuss her programme for the first half of June with her. Here is her diary of engagements:

Sunday, June 1st. Fly to London. Dorchester Hotel.
Monday, June 2nd. Open new fashion department, Harrods. 11 am.
Tuesday, June 3rd. Appear at the fashion trade ball at the Savoy Hotel.
Wednesday, June 4th. Fly to Munich. Fashion show.
Thursday, June 5th. Return to London.
Friday, June 6th. Attend film premiere. Odeon, Leicester Square.
Saturday, June 7th. Visit hospital for sick children.
Sunday, June 8th. Free.
Monday, June 9th. Fly to New York.
Tuesday, June 10th. Appear on TV chat show.
Wednesday, June 11th. Discuss new advertising campaign. Moonlight shampoo.
Thursday, June 12th. Fly to Paris.
Friday, June 13th. Make personal appearance at new restaurant.
Saturday, June 14th. Appear on French television.

MISS WORLD   OK. What are we doing in June?
YOU   Well, on Sunday, 1st June, we're flying to London.
MISS WORLD   Where are we staying?
YOU   At the Dorchester Hotel.

Work in pairs and continue in the same way.

LISTENING ACTIVITIES

You are going to hear a typical British news broadcast.
Listen carefully.

E   Listen and write:

1 The Queen _____ _____ in Australia on an official visit.
2 The Football Association _____ _____ _____ investigate
  violence during _____ .
3 The Prime Minister _____ _____ members of the Girl
  Guides Association.
4 The police _____ _____ _____ higher pay.
5 And finally, Miss World is _____ _____ .

✳ **Listen and choose:**

	now	the future
1 Australia _____		
2 At a meeting yesterday, _____		
3 The Prime Minister _____		
4 The Police Federation _____		
5 Miss World, _____		

READING COMPREHENSION

Dear George,

Thank you for your card. I am glad you're having a good
time, but I am not surprised. Provence is wonderful at
this time of year.

We are going on holiday next month. I like to take my
summer holiday late, then winter does not seem quite so
long. We are going to St Ives, in Cornwall. I have an
aunt there, so we can stay with her.

We are not taking the car. We are going by train. There
is so much traffic on the roads in the summer that driving
is no pleasure and we want to do a lot of walking. I am
taking my fishing rod and Belinda is planning to do some
painting.

Love, *Chris and Belinda*

F   Questions

1 Where is George and what is he doing?
2 Where are Chris and Belinda going?
3 Who are they going to stay with?
4 Why does ~~George~~ CHRIS prefer to have his holiday in September?
5 Why isn't he taking the car?
6 Why do you think Chris is taking his fishing rod?
7 What is Belinda going to do?

GRAMMAR SUMMARY

G   We often use the *present continuous* **as a future when arrangements are fixed.**

Examples: Frank's getting married.
            Who's he marrying?
            I'm not going to the wedding.

Statements

I'm		
You're		
He/she's	flying	to Paris tomorrow.
We're You're They're		

Questions

Am I		
Are you		
Is he/she	flying	to Paris tomorrow?
we Are you they		

Negatives

I'm			
You're			
He/she's	not	going	by train.
We're You're They're			

H   Your friends, Tom and Iris, have booked a holiday near Monte Carlo.

1 Ask if they are taking their car.
2 Ask if they are going by train.
3 Ask when they are leaving.
4 Find out how long they are staying there.
5 Find out which hotel they are staying at.
6 Ask if Tom is taking his movie camera.
7 Ask if they are taking their money in traveller's cheques.
8 Find out when they are coming back.

HOMEWORK EXERCISES

A   A friend tells you that he/she is going abroad.

Ask questions:

1 Find out where he/she is going.
2 Find out when your friend is going.
3 Find out why he/she is going.
4 Find out how long your friend is going for.
5 Find out if he/she is going to pay his/her own fare.

B   You are the personal manager of a famous pop musician called Rocky Valentine. Here is his diary of engagements for the next week.

Sunday:	Free.	
Monday:	10am:	Rehearsal, London.
	7pm:	Live television broadcast.
Tuesday:	11am:	Fly to Frankfurt, Kronenburg Hotel.
Wednesday:	10am:	Rehearsal.
	8pm:	Frankfurt Concert.
Thursday:	2pm:	Fly to Stockholm.
Friday:	8pm:	Stockholm Concert.
Saturday:	10am:	Fly to London.
	8pm:	London Concert.

Use the information in the diary to complete the conversation below:

ROCKY   OK. Let's go over the plans for next week. Are we working on Sunday?

YOU   _____

ROCKY   Fine and what time does the rehearsal start on Monday?

YOU   _____

ROCKY   And we're appearing on television on Monday night. What time do you think we'll finish?

YOU   _____

ROCKY And what's happening on Tuesday?
YOU   _____
ROCKY Where are we staying?
YOU   _____
ROCKY Oh fine. We stayed there once before, didn't we?
YOU   _____
ROCKY And we're doing the Frankfurt Concert in the evening. When are we flying to Stockholm?
YOU   _____
ROCKY But we aren't doing a concert in Stockholm on Thursday evening, are we?
YOU   _____
ROCKY Thank goodness for that; and when are we coming back to London?
YOU   _____
ROCKY Oh, that's great. We'll be able to go and see the Arsenal–Tottenham game!

C Dictation

We are going to Scotland for our holiday. We are leaving early on Saturday morning and I hope we will get to York about 11 o'clock.

We are spending the night in York, then on Sunday we are driving up to Scotland. We are going to stay at a lovely little hotel near a lake. Of course we will probably get some rain, but I am sure we will have a fantastic holiday.

STUDY THE WORDS

Remember these words (look at the Dialogue):

Entertainment:

film premiere	engagement
fashion ball	rehearsal
disco	great
chat show	drummer
pop group	appearance

Other words in this unit (can you find them?):

art historian	surprised
aunt	relaxing
fishing rod	pleasure
shampoo	artist

1 Look at these verbs and read the questions and statements. Put a circle round the letter for the missing verb.

A has   **B** is   **C** shall   **D** will

1 Who _____ getting married?   A B C D

2 Can you tell me how long it _____ take?   A B C D

3 George _____ had an accident.   A B C D

4 _____ I send him some flowers?   A B C D

5 _____ you answer the telephone?   A B C D

6 Where _____ we go this evening?   A B C D

7 He _____ going on holiday next month.   A B C D

8 Chris _____ just bought a new car.   A B C D

9 How much _____ it cost?   A B C D

10 _____ he got the tickets?   A B C D

2 Write what you could say in these situations:

1 Your camera is broken. You want the assistant to have a look at it.
You say: _____ ?

2 You want an estimate to repair the camera.
You say: _____ ?

3 You want to go swimming with your friend. Suggest it.
You say: _____ ?

4 You are telephoning. You want to speak to your friend, Helen.
You say: _____ ?

5 Your friend is thirsty. You offer to make some tea.
You say: _____ ?

3 Look at the words on the left. Then look at the words on the right and try to find the words that belong together. Then write sentences like the examples:

Examples:

A doctor   pass a driving test
Drivers   pass examinations

You write:

A doctor *has to* pass examinations.
Drivers *have to* pass a driving test.

Now you do it.

Soldiers   work at night
A teacher   look at passports
Immigration officers   correct homework
Children   go to school
A hospital nurse   wear uniforms

1 _____

2 _____

3 _____

4 _____

5 _____

4 Read this story about my sister's party. Then find words to put in the empty spaces.

My sister is _____ a party on Saturday. She hasn't _____ many people. She is _____ some records from John, and I am _____ her some records. My mother is _____ all the food. What an easy party!